BEVERLEY
BEFORE I FORGET

by
David E. Warnes

Highgate of Beverley

Highgate Publications (Beverley) Limited
1999

Acknowledgements:
All of the photographs published were taken either by the author or members of his family, with the exception of the school photograph, which was taken by Geo. Holdsworth Ltd. of Hartlepool, and the photograph of the Hall Garth, which was found among the effects of my uncle, the late Mr. Laurie Parker. Efforts to contact Geo. Holdsworth have proved in vain, as have efforts to identify the photographer of the Hall Garth. I am happy to acknowledge both contributions, and am grateful to both parties. The photographs which involve the Regal Cinema were taken by the author when on an assignment given him by the late Mr. Sandy Lewis, and I should like to place on record my gratitude to him.

A proportion of the proceeds from the sale of this book will be donated by the author to The Alzheimer's Disease Society, Gordon House, 10 Greencoat Place, London, SW1P 1PH.

British Library Cataloguing in Publication Data.
A catalogue record for this book is available from the British Library.

© 1999 David E. Warnes

ISBN 1 902645 09 x

Published for David E. Warnes by

Highgate of Beverley

Highgate Publications (Beverley) Limited
24 Wylies Road, Beverley, HU17 7AP. Telephone (01482) 866826

Produced by

baprint

4 Newbegin. Lairgate, Beverley, HU17 8EG. Telephone (01482) 886017

'There was a time when meadow, grove, and stream,
The earth and every common sight, to me did seem
Apparelled in celestial light,
The glory and the freshness of a dream.
It is not now as it hath been of yore;
Turn wheresoe'er I may, by night or day,
The things which I have seen I now can see no more.'

William Wordsworth

***This book is dedicated to my parents.
Bless 'em.***

Preface

The gift of retirement came to me in October 1997. It was a gift of the opportunities that in a very busy working life I simply did not have the time to grasp. However, since my retirement I have visited Beverley on business, social, and recreational occasions, and have found the time to stand and stare. Whilst being aware of the many changes that have taken place over the years, and indeed are still taking place, it is only recently that I have realised just how monumental and far reaching those changes have been. I have, therefore, taken one of the opportunities afforded me to recall some of the Beverley I knew in the 1940s, 1950s, and early 1960s. Many long established institutions and businesses have completely disappeared from the scene, many are so changed as to be unrecognisable, and others are about to be lost for ever. Some may say that this is the price of progress, but I feel that many may well have questioned the price they paid.

From my early childhood to my mid-Twenties I lived in Beverley, knowing many of the streets, the houses, the people, the schools, the churches, some of the public houses, and much of the surrounding countryside. Briefly recalling those early years, then, is the subject of this little book. Taking some of the streets of Beverley that I knew in those far-off days, and remembering them as they were for me, together with some of the people who were such an integral part of the scene. Remembering too some of the local countryside as it was then.

I have deliberately avoided serious research lest recollection is impoverished by fact, so all that follows are very personal memories and anecdotes, which may well have lost some accuracies with the passing of time, but I truly feel they were worth recording, because for me many of those memories remain as clear as the time recalled, and the people of that time are all remembered with much affection. Beverley today is so much changed, and some of that change I know has been inevitable; nevertheless, in remembering those times I feel that I am recalling an age of innocence, an age of contentment, a carefree age where I would have been happy if time had stood still. Alas, time has gone on, but this is how it was for me in Beverley long ago. I know that I was indeed fortunate and privileged to have been there.

CHAPTER ONE

Eastgate, Highgate and Wednesday Market

We lived in Eastgate, from 1938 to 1963, at number 26, one of two Georgian houses opposite the offices of Armstrong's Patents. Armstrong's factory covered much of the eastern side of this thoroughfare, producing armaments during the war years, and car parts latterly. I recall playing football and cricket on what we called 'Armstrong's Front', which was the concrete frontage opposite number 26. The factory was, I remember, somewhat noisy, and many is the time the street rang to the sound of steel rods being offloaded at the factory gate. You could also hear the sound of 'Music While You Work' over the noise of the machinery inside the factory. Today not one vestige of Armstrong's factory remains, with almost the whole site being given over to housing. I am sure, however, that Armstrong's contribution to the local economy will be remembered by many Beverley people.

It is difficult to believe it now, but Eastgate then was part of the main Hull to York trunk road, with not much traffic in those early days, and it seemed to me that a good deal of it was horse drawn. For instance, the regular Ringtons tea deliveries were done by pony and two-wheeled cab and Dick Malton delivered fruit and vegetables by horse and rully. Occasionally the cry of 'Round Again!' would be heard, heralding a visit by the local rag and bone man as he pushed his old pram from street to street. He was known throughout the town as 'Round Again', and I wonder if anyone ever knew his real name? Our local coalman was Mr. Towse, who delivered from his premises in nearby Trinity Lane.

Taking the Armstrong's side of Eastgate and heading towards its junction with Friars Lane, I recall Glenton's furniture stores. Mr. Glenton, who always wore a trilby hat, was often to be seen standing in the shop doorway. Next came a small grocery shop, this was I think Miss Locking's, then it was Mr. Dickinson's, subsequently Mr Atkinson's and finally it was run by a baker, Mr. Littlefair. I was often sent on errands to this shop, and also to the establishment next door, which was Mr. Wood's dairy. I would be sent there with a huge white jug for the milk, which Mr. Wood's daughter Betty would fill from a large silver churn. I used to think

Armstrong's front. c.1952

The author in the garden of No. 26 Eastgate 1941.

it funny that I never saw any cows there, even though that was where our milk came from. Further along from Wood's was Dickie Care's Eastgate Market, a fairly large grocery shop, where the aroma of hams, nutmeg, coffee and other provisions filled the air. I would gaze in wonderment at Cyril operating the manual bacon slicer. This particular establishment had a shop window system that allowed small boys, and indeed adults if they were so minded, to stand close to where the two panes of glass met, raise an arm and a leg from the same side of the body, thus giving a reflective impression of flying. Harry Worth used this ploy to good effect in the opening sequence of his TV show.

Down from Care's and past a row of cottages on the corner of Friars Lane was Mr. Robson's plumber's shop. Mrs. Robson used a part of this shop to sell antiques and second-hand goods. The bulk of my stuffed bird and animal collection came from Mrs. Robson's emporium, much of my pocket money being spent there. Mention of Friars Lane brings to mind the small farm at the bottom of the lane owned by the Jackson family. Mr. Jackson was a large jovial chap, always dressed in a brown overall coat, with a flat cap and generally carrying a stick. I recall that, as small boys, we would watch the animals from the nearby railway bridge, being very mindful of the dogs. That little farm was mainly pigs, but I remember chickens, goats and a cow or two. I also recall the 'good farmyard' smells at that end of Friars Lane.

Heading back now to Armstrong's Factory, and going towards Wednesday Market on the same side of the road, I recall the Oddfellows Arms at the Trinity Lane junction, I believe Mr. Puttnam was the landlord. Next, just across the road was a fish and chip shop. I do not remember the proprietor, only that it seemed to change owners quite often. It was, however, good for the odd 'two penn'orth' of chips. Then came Mrs. Watkin's shop, which was a good little shop from a small boy's point of view. For a penny you could get a fizzy drink called Vantas. This came in all sorts of bright colours and was made to order in a small glass bottle with a screw top. Liquorice root could be purchased here, and I am sure too that you could obtain, in a conical shaped paper bag, a pennyworth of Kali [I am not too sure of the spelling of this particular product], a white powder, which when touched with a licked finger and applied to the mouth would fizz and turn yellow. I think it was a kind of sherbet, only cheaper and much more fun. I think Mrs. Watkin also ran a small popular library. Going on from Mrs. Watkin's shop then were a number of houses which led up to the final shop on that side of Eastgate, which was not of much interest to me, but I think it traded in ladies' fashion, hats and such like.

Crossing Eastgate at its junction with Wednesday Market and heading down the western side of the street we would pass a row of terraced houses before coming to what we called Blizzard's Arch, which was directly opposite Armstrong's factory. This arch led to George and Dragon Yard, with, I think, three cottages in it, which in turn led to Blizzard's Passage which ran through to Highgate via the George and Dragon pub precincts. Mrs. Gibson and her family lived in one of the cottages and I can vividly remember all the Union Jacks and bunting, together with a huge banner declaring 'Welcome home Sid' that marked the return from the war of one of her sons. Blizzard's Passage was seldom closed and I can tell you it was a very useful short-cut. Next came a row of small cottages followed by two Georgian houses. I lived at number 26 for all of my childhood and beyond. I have many memories of that house and most of them are happy.

However, one particularly frightening episode remains with me which took place during the war. I would have been about three years old at the time, and I can remember my mother finding a mouse in the house and her being so scared that she called our neighbour from number 24 for help. Mrs. Campey, a good neighbour if ever there was one, came round with Henry, her large and well fed ginger tomcat. Henry was duly left to hunt for the mouse, and things returned to normal. I had been put to bed, and all the blinds in the house had been drawn down, as it was the wartime blackout. It was well after dark when I was suddenly awakened by the sound of the blind in my bedroom flapping violently against the window, and I could see the stars through huge tears that were appearing in it. My terrified screaming awoke my parents who rushed in to find Henry the cat trying to get out. Apparently he had not been too keen on mouse hunting and must have fallen asleep in my bedroom. I can also remember watching as part of Armstrong's factory went up in flames one night. It seemed that a long time elapsed before the Fire Brigade had the blaze under control, and the crowd cheered the first jet of water. I cannot leave number 26 without a brief mention of the apple tree which stood in the garden. Every year it produced a bountiful crop of Keswick cooking apples. The variety, Keswick, is seldom heard of today, so if that dear old

Father harvesting the Keswicks at number 26. c.1951.

tree is still around I am sure it will be a rarity. I hope that it is still there.

Next door to our house, at Number 28 lived Miss Hewson. I can well remember this lady as she was the School Attendance Officer. She seemed always to be dressed in a mauve-coloured, floor-length skirt and cape, and invariably wore a hat with a veil. I can recall her standing at the teacher's desk, in front of the class at Minster Boys School and calling the register, using a lorgnette. Her role was perhaps linked up with that of Mr. Fox, who was known as the 'kid catcher'. Miss Hewson, as I remember, was somewhat reclusive, and her house and garden had suffered a kind of genteel neglect, that, as in later years I was to become acquainted with the works of Dickens, I would compare my memories of her with his Miss Havisham. Alas, there was no Estella.

On then from Miss Hewson's were the gardens belonging to some houses in Highgate. One of them belonged to Mr. Fidling, who had some pear trees in his garden. They were sampled on many occasions by us youngsters. Next, and almost opposite Glenton's was a small garage where a chap called Inman repaired cars and motorcycles. Mrs. Winter's house was next. I can remember her very well as she sold lemonade and other mineral drinks from her house. Later she moved to Railway Street, and then to Minster Moorgate, always selling lemonade. Further along was Wilf Taylor's barber's shop. Mr. Taylor was a skilled craftsman, and many interesting conversations were listened to as one waited one's turn, some becoming clearer to me as I grew older. The next business premises were Brentano's cycle and motorcycle repair shop. I can remember well the smell of the oil, grease, and paraffin which they also sold. Mrs. Brentano, who I think was also a schoolteacher, often served in the shop, and always seemed to know just which size brake blocks or cotter pins you needed to keep your bike on the road. They were very helpful people. Finally in Eastgate there were rows of small cottages which ran down as far as the front door of the Vicarage, which in those days I am sure was in Eastgate.

Eastgate area friends remembered are Peter Moore, Philip Thompson, Philip Evans, Mavis Nightingale, Delia Whitteron, Jimmy Mcevoy, Ron Atkinson, Neville Dickinson, Rosamund Hargreaves, Pat and Jeff Collins, and Michael Collier.

Now to Highgate. This street of stone setts runs from Wednesday Market to the north door of the Minster, of which much more later. Taking the west side and heading down towards the Minster from Lord Roberts Road, the first few properties were probably officially in Wednesday Market, but I always thought of them as being in Highgate. I can remember Myers' antique shop, which I believe also served as a café. This is now an estate agent's. Next came some large terraced houses. The Goldthorpe family I think lived in one of these, and also Mr. John Long, the Minster Organist and Choirmaster, and his family lived in one. Going further on I recall a row of small terraced houses. I can recall some of the people who lived in them, but I particularly remember one gentleman who dealt in ferrets, rabbits, and guinea pigs. These were very interesting things to a small boy, and if I had been given the choice I might well have purchased a ferret from this gentleman. However, in the interest of family harmony I opted for a rabbit. He was a big man with ginger hair and a moustache who always wore a spotted red necktie, and a flat cap. I cannot remember his name. Next came the curate's house, and I think the only curate I can recall living there was Mr. Brownrigg, but I'm sure there would be more. Moving further along was a row of medium-sized terraced houses before a small grocery and bakery shop. I think that this shop was owned by the Watson's. Next came the Minster Girls School playground which ran down as far as Highgate's junction with Minster Moorgate. This now serves as a car park.

Crossing the road, and going back towards Wednesday Market on the east side of Highgate there was a row of small terraced houses, my uncle and aunt living in one of these, before coming to Mr. Charlie Lucas's barber's shop. This is where I had my first haircut. I remember Mr. Lucas as a very smart gentleman, almost bald but with black hair and sideburns. I can remember he wore armlets on his shirt sleeves, and a black apron. I went there with my Grandad. While we were waiting I remember Mr. Lucas sharpening his cut-throat razor on a leather strap. When it came to my turn, because I was small, Mr. Lucas placed a stool on the seat of the barber's chair for me to sit on. Mrs. Lucas used to sweep up the hair and make cups of tea. I did not take too kindly to my first haircut. Mr. Roy Forth later took on this business and it remained a hairdresser's for quite some time before it became a teashop and café. Next I remember Mr. Witty the plumber had his shop, which was later owned by Mr. Pexton.

View of Highgate showing Osgerby's coachworks and the old pump on the right. c.1953.

Going on from the plumber's we come to Osgerby's the coachbuilders. These premises were quite large, and were a mainly wooden construction. An archway led through them into a small courtyard with some small cottages at the rear. There was a hansom cab parked under the archway, and I can remember that I often played in it. At that time coach building no longer took place, and the property was somewhat derelict, but my Uncle Fred, who owned the place, used part of the workshop to repair bicycles. I used to roam all over that old coachworks, and I recall that Uncle Fred had other responsibilities too, as he was the Minster Steeplekeeper, which involved being in charge of bellringing, and maintenance of the Minster clock. He was a kind man, and never charged a deal for repairing cycles. I believe that the old coachworks was eventually gently dismantled and taken to the Castle Museum in York where it was reassembled as an exhibit. Just outside the coachworks and on the pavement to the left as one would have entered it stood a large cast-iron manual water pump and trough. I can remember this pump being in full working order.

Continuing on towards Wednesday Market there was a row of large terrace houses, before coming to the George and Dragon public house, the entrance to which was from the passage which ran through to Eastgate. The entrance to the inn was on the right of the passage, with the public house services to the left, much as it is today, only it is no longer the George and Dragon. The first landlord I can recall was Mr. Stabler, and the last was Mr. Ben Coates. I was too young to avail myself of their services. There then followed a row of mixed terrace houses, and I recall that Mr. Gilbert Gawan lived in one of the large ones. I recall that Mr. Gawan sang in the Minster Choir, and was well known for that, and for his work in Sudan. Those then are my memories of Highgate.

Wednesday Market is a sort of triangular affair, which can be described as funnelling into Butcher Row. Taking the side crossing Railway Street from Eastgate, I remember the first shop was Reynold's department store, which sold everything from clothing to furniture. I can recall Mr. Frost, the proprietor, and his staff having the old-fashioned courtesies you seldom see today. Next came Sugden's paper shop. That is what we called it then; I suppose that it would be a newsagent's now. I used to be dispatched to Sugden's to 'pay the papers'. This shop I think eventually became the Fiveways Cafe. Then there was, and still is to this day, Peck's the gamedealer and fishmonger. In those days the pheasants, hares, and other game used to hang outside the shop. This is one of the few businesses in the town which I think have survived in the same family for all those years. Rudd's came next as I recall, and I think it specialised in such things as pork pies etc. Anyway, I remember a stone figure of a happy pig stood on its hind legs in the window. I think it was painted an orange colour. Then came the Queen's Head public house, followed by a passage known as Tindall Alley. Now just a few dozen yards down this passage was a derelict printing works where we young lads would go to find the metal typesetts which were strewn around. These were small rectangular pieces of metal with a reverse letter or number at one end . If you found enough you could make all sorts of words with them. There was Mr. George Miles' barber's shop next, followed by Miss Leighton's greengrocery shop, later to become Laughton's.

Still in Wednesday Market, and across its junction with Butcher Row the butcher's shop known as Ye Olde Porke Shoppe is still owned by the same family, the Hillman's, as it was all those years ago. My grandparents always referred to it as 'Spotted Cow', which was its name when, well before my time, it was a public house. Next to this butcher's I can remember a Wesleyan Chapel, which was demolished to make way for Crystal Motors car sales and repairs, which extended through into Well Lane. This has since been replaced by Boyes Department Store. On the corner of Lord Roberts Road was a gas showroom. Finally, between its junctions with Eastgate and Highgate there was Mr. Redhead's taxi office, and also Mr. Neal's the plumber's showrooms. His business was advertised in huge black letters on the outside white-washed wall. Although a market is now held in Wednesday Market, I can never recall one being held during my childhood.

CHAPTER TWO

Butcher Row, Toll Gavel and Saturday Market

My early recollections of the main shopping thoroughfares of Beverley concentrate mainly on those establishments which were of interest to a small boy. I am aware too, that in recalling such a concentrated area of retail activity, some businesses will have either preceded, or superseded others. That for me is incidental, the important thing is that they are remembered. Both Butcher Row and Toll Gavel were main streets, and traffic flowed through them in both directions, although I do recall that Butcher Row and part of Toll Gavel were given to a one-way system, perhaps some time in the early Fifties. At the Wednesday Market end of Butcher Row, I can recall Mr. Arthur Duffill's gentlemen's outfitters, followed by Goldthorpe's, the chemist. Mr. Goldthorpe was a white-haired old gentleman, with a white moustache, and rosy cheeks. His special flu mixture was much in demand in the winter months, and must have been very efficacious as coughs and colds soon seemed to clear up. I recall the Mayfair tobacconist's and sweet shop, which was run by Mr. Geoff Kemp. I think that now it is a toyshop, although still in the same family. There were many different brands of cigarettes in those days, most of which as young men we tried out. I can remember Turf, Robin, Players Weights, Senior Service, Park Drive, Wills Woodbines, Strand, Passing Cloud, State Express, Kensitas, Players Bachelor, Gold Leaf, and, 'for your throat's sake', Craven A. I wonder how many of those brands are still available today.

Opposite Well Lane was the Marble Arch Cinema. This was run by Mr. Harry Popple, a jocular man, always very smart, in fact I think he always wore a dinner jacket and bow tie when the cinema was open. The children's Saturday morning film shows were always well attended, and cost only 3d. The programme always had a cartoon and a serial which always ended with the hero in an impossible situation so that you would be sure to 'come back next week' to see how he escaped. Always in black and white, the films featured Tom Mix, Gene Autry, Roy Rogers and Trigger, Zorro, Old Mother Riley, not forgetting Kitty, Laurel and Hardy, the Three Stooges. and many many more, and, of course, Tarzan. How we all cheered the 'goodies' and booed the 'baddies' as fortunes changed on the screen. Occasionally the reel would break, which resulted in a concerted groan, followed by a small riot until order was restored as the film resumed. At the end of each show dozens of small boys would be released running and shouting onto the street, with the index and second fingers of their right hands formed in the shape of a pistol, and their left hands slapping their backsides, as they became for that moment in time their cowboy heroes, and fought those battles again on the way home. Yes, they were very happy days at the Marble Arch. Two films which attracted large audiences to the Marble Arch were *The Blue Lamp,* which starred Jack Warner, and *The Wicked Lady,* with Margaret Lockwood. I think that all three cinemas in Beverley were open every night apart from Sundays. They also did matinee performances on Saturdays.

Next along from the cinema was Gresswell's furniture store. This was a large store, on two floors. I can remember Mr. Gresswell Snr. riding to work on his bicycle. He was always very smart in black jacket, striped trousers, bowtie, Homberg hat and cigar, with his cycle clips neatly in place. Mr. Gresswell's three sons managed the shop. They were Mr. Fred, Mr. Ernest and Mr. Jack. I recall that next came the D & F electrical shop. I can remember that it would be jokingly called 'Diddlum and Fiddlum', but I think that the D & F stood for Fogg and Davies. I know that Mr. Davies, the proprietor, became a mayor of Beverley. Our first FM radio came from D & F, and, when it closed down, the Yorkshire Electricity Board took it over as a showroom. Mr. Cattle's second-hand shop was on the corner of Wilbert Lane. Now this was an interesting shop to me, always having some stuffed birds for sale. I can remember that Mrs. Grice, who I think was Mr. Cattle's sister, always drove a hard bargain, and I was not successful in all my dealings, but then my finances were somewhat limited. However, there was no charge for browsing. Mr. Cattle used to make and repair cooking pots and pans. Just across Wilbert Lane and opposite Mr. Cattle's was, and still is, the Angel public house, and I can remember as a boy hearing much singing and merriment coming from within. In later times a contemporary of mine, Les Arundale, was the landlord for quite a few years.

Opposite Gresswell's was Mr. Ringrose, the butcher, and then there was Mr. Carling, the tailor, whose little shop was followed by Sanderson's the greengrocers. Now Sanderson's was owned by Mr. and Mrs. Don Constable who both worked in the shop, along with

Mrs. Coulbeck, who assisted them. I was a part-time delivery boy at this shop for a while. The deliveries took place in the morning, and I can remember having a special bicycle with a big wheel at the back and a very small one at the front. This was to accommodate a large metal framework in which to place the orders for delivery. I loved this little job, until Mr. Constable got the contract to supply lettuce to the Beverley Grammar School canteen. I was at the time a pupil at that school, and I can remember doing my best to deliver those lettuces especially early, before my fellow pupils began to arrive at the school. I was most concerned that some ridicule would follow my progress up the school drive on that bike. It didn't help too that I had also to cycle past the Headmaster's house. The next shop was a little sweet shop which seemed to have several different proprietors over the years, but I remember that Mr. Jack Ramsden ran it for a good few years. Also opposite Gresswell's was, and still is to this day, Peck's fish and chip shop. When I first went to Peck's I couldn't see over the counter, but I can remember Mr. Jack Peck doing the frying while Mrs. Peck served. The wonderful thing about Peck's is that it is one of the few unchanged things about Beverley. It is still in the same family, the third generation to my knowledge. The fish and chips still taste as good as they did all those years ago, and I make a point of having 'one of each' on my visits to the town. Long may they continue.

I can just recall that the butcher's shop next to Peck's was Mr. Fussey's, which then became Mr. Harold Robinson's and still is owned and run by his son Peter, although, as I write, Peter has decided to retire and close the business after more than 50 years service to the people of Beverley, so another change will be seen there. The Tudor Café was next, and Mr. Peabody's the gentlemen's outfitter was just along from there, probably where Brooke's store is today. White's papershop was just opposite the Angel. Mr. White was Scottish. I did quite a stint there delivering both morning and evening newspapers. My round was the Grovehill Road area. I enjoyed that little job, and remember Arty English, a fellow paper lad, showing me the ropes in my first week. The pay was ten shillings a week, and when you got that ten bob note at the end of the week you were well pleased. What was White's is now the Beverley Bookshop.

Just along from White's paper shop there was a wet fish shop which I think was Mainprize's, and thereabouts was a cobbler called Braithwaite. Frank Dee, the grocer, and Atkinson, the jeweller, were also in that area, and opposite Atkinson's was a wool shop and milliner called Ashelford's. I also have a recollection of a greengrocer called Burnett close by. There were two sweet shops that I well remember. They were at opposite sides of the road. One was the Minster Chocolate Box, which also sold toys, so it was often visited by us young lads. Mr. Mercer was the proprietor. The other sweet shop was Cherry's, and I can recall that most of our family's wartime sweet ration came from Mr. Joe Cherry's shop. Those two ounces of Smarties once a week were eagerly awaited. Mr. Bielby's fruit and vegetable shop was close to the Minster Chocolate Box. Now somewhere between Mr. Cherry's and Ashelford's was Harrison's bicycle shop. I have reason to remember this shop because on one of our family holidays, when I would have been about eleven years old, we stopped for refreshments at Beckhole on the North Yorkshire moors. It was there that we met a very elderly gentleman who lived in a small cottage next to the little inn. It turned out that he was called Harrison, and that he was a close relative of the people who ran the shop. During the week of our holiday I got to know the old gentleman quite well. He was 80-years-old and had spent much of his life studying and collecting butterflies and moths. That week I learned much about his work and he was really pleased to meet people from his home town.

And now to turn to Toll Gavel. Marson and Wood's shoe shop, which has recently closed down, was there when I was a boy, but just opposite was, I believe, a draper's shop. This was Uriah Butter's, and to a small boy this was an interesting place. I remember that the floors were wooden, and I can recall two black pot-bellied stoves at either end of the ground floor. But the real point of interest was the mechanical payment system. When cash was given for any particular item purchased, it would be placed by the shop assistant into a small round metal container, which would then whizz on a wire to an office, which seemed to be in the roof. A receipt and any change due would whizz back down the wire to be given to the buyer. I was much intrigued by all this, particularly on busy days. I think that Spink's the chemist occupied this site for some time before it became a conglomeration of smaller shops.

Hutton's Electrical shop was next. I can recall that Mr. Hutton was a well-known local golfer. I also seem to remember that Pottage's ironmonger's was located there, although they also had a branch in Cross Street, which ran independently. Then there was Mitchell's. I recall that this shop served as both a toy shop and a tobacconist's. My own particular interests here were the model aircraft, Dinky toys, and Meccano. Mr. Mitchell was very patient with us, as limited funds meant long periods of browsing before buying.

There was a Stead and Simpson's shoe shop on the corner of Register Square, now Skelton's baker's and confectioner's. Mr. Haigh was the manager as I recall. Opposite the shoe shop was Booth's, the butcher's. Mr. Clive Booth, the owner, was a well-known clay pigeon shot, and represented England. What is now Dixon's was Atkinson's paper shop, or newsagent's as it would be called today. I remember the Cooperative Wholesale Society, or the Co-op, occupied most of one side of Register Square and around the corner into Toll Gavel. It was quite a large affair with groceries and a chemist's. The Army and Navy stores were next to Atkinson's, followed by Curry's electrical shop. Woolworth's, or F. W. Woolworth as it was known as then, although it will always be called 'Woolie's', is still on the same site as it was all those years ago, though much changed. The wooden floors and the display counters, each sectioned off with its particular product and its own helpful shopgirl, are well remembered. Woolworth's seemed to have everything, from ironmongery to perfume, from confectionery to electrical goods. It even had its own distinctive and welcoming odour, something akin to roasting peanuts mingled with biscuits, other confectionery and floor polish. The cashier occupied a glass-panelled office at the far end of the store. I also recall the exit into the passage that led through to Walkergate was at the far end opposite the cashier's office.

Across the road, opposite F. W. Woolworth, I can remember Burton's wallpaper and paint shop, which was next to Ibbotson's the tobacconist's. Ibbotson's had a life-size wooden figure of a red Indian just inside the door, which was rather interesting to a small boy. I wonder where it is now? I can recall all the jars of different tobacco in the window, from thick black twist to the fine golden strands of light Virginia. I can remember seeing the blue paper packets of Punch tobacco on display, along with tins of Three Nuns, St. Julien, Whisky Flake, and St. Bruno. I think that Punch was a locally produced tobacco. There was also a large choice of pipes displayed. My Grandad was a pipe smoker and often took me into Ibbotson's with him. Mr. Turner was the proprietor. Although in later life I tried to smoke a pipe, I didn't really take to it, as the sensation of actually smoking the pipe did not in any way live up to the promised fragrances which issued from the fresh tobacco.

The Lichfield Hotel stood where the Halifax Building Society now stands. I think that Mrs. Madge Battersby was the landlady. Later she took the licence of the Windmill in Lairgate. Noel White's the gentlemen's outfitter was then located on the corner of Landress Lane. Just along from there was Schofield's department store. Now this store had a department which specialised in school uniforms, and I can well remember the interruptions to the summer holidays, when I would be taken reluctantly to be kitted out for the start of a new school year. Miss Kitty Campey was one of the very helpful ladies who made this event more palatable. Latterly Miss Campey assisted at Strefford's the gentlemen's outfitter in Saturday Market. I can remember that Selles the chemist's was just further along. They had a photographic section, and Mr. Fletcher, the manager, gave me lots of assistance and advice when it came to the purchase of things photographic.

Other retail emporia recalled in the Toll Gavel area are Benefit Shoe shop, Myton Textiles, Gallon's, Maypole, and Baggs. The latter three shops were all grocers. I cannot precisely remember their exact position, but again that subtle aroma of coffee, spices and hams is brought to mind when recalling them. Latterly in Toll Gavel there were two of the first supermarkets in Beverley, William Jackson's and Goodfellow's, both now gone. Montague Burton the tailor occupied the same site as it does today, although the tailoring side has gone, and it is now just plain Burton's. Then the place exuded quality, with its parquet floors, oak panelling and mirrors together with the unique almost insulated atmosphere afforded by the many bales of cloth. It was quite special buying a suit from Montague Burton in those days: choosing the cloth and the style, being measured, and returning for fittings before finally getting your suit. I have observed with some sadness the transition over the years of this fine tailoring service to its present day trendiness and obsession with youth. Above Burton's in most towns in those days you would find a billiard and snooker hall, and the Beverley Burton's was no exception. When the billiard hall closed down, in the late Fifties I think it was, the first Chinese restaurant to be opened in Beverley took its place.

Saturday Market holds many memories. Mills and Sowerby's wine and spirit shop, where one would be served by Mr. Ernest Mills. Thirsk's agricultural stores was where the Market Cross

Mill's wine and spirits shop. c.1952.

Newsagency, formerly Hatfield's, is now. I can remember often going to Thirsk's for a stone of 'Balancer meal' for the few chickens we kept at home. This was a fine powdered meal which seemed to weigh heavy, particularly when conveyed home on the handlebars of a not too steady bicycle. All the assistants at Thirsk's wore brown coat-type overalls. I can recall Mr. Eric Wainwright was one of the staff. Another agricultural store on the edge of the Market Place, probably just in Ladygate, was Holtby's. We would buy hay and straw and food for our pet rabbits and guinea pigs there.

Akrill's the Gunsmith's is still there today, much as it was all those years past, although I can recall the name above the door being H. Esau Akrill, and Mr. Geoff Akrill and his brother serving in the shop. I can remember that as young lads we would buy our catapult elastic from Akrill's. You could get it in three sizes, sparrow, starling or crow, but most of us generally used starling. Modern times, I suppose, have slightly limited the window displays to what we see today. In other words, one can no longer admire the quality and the craftsmanship of the guns so closely. I can remember Richmond's sweets and icecream shop was in the same row and would often be visited before going to The Picture Playhouse, the former Corn Exchange which was always a cinema in my time. It was run by Mr. Ernest Symmons, who was a keen local cinematographer, and later by his wife, Mrs. Thelma Symmons. The Playhouse had an atmosphere all of its own. As the smallest cinema in Beverley, it was probably the warmest, and one seemed to be closer to the action on the screen. The double seats on the stairs to each side of the small balcony gave the occupants the feeling of having the place to themselves, and were much in demand by the courting couples of the day. I can recall seeing such films as *Scott of the Antarctic*, and *Henry V*, at The Playhouse. Stirring stuff in those days. It is good to see that The Playhouse is still in use today, concentrating more on live shows, although I know that films are still shown from time to time.

I well remember the Rambla Bakery, Café and Confectionery Shop. This was a large enterprise, and very popular in the town. It was located next to the Green Dragon public house. The bakery delivered produce around the town and local villages using small three-wheeler vans painted in the distinctive orange livery that made the Rambla vans such a welcome sight. The business was owned by Mr. Stanley Stephenson and his family. I have reason to be grateful to him for the help and encouragement he gave to a young man's interest in photography. I sometimes wonder how such an integral part of Beverley, as the Rambla enterprise surely was, can have faded from the scene, but then so much has gone over the years.

The Dandy Tuck Shop was close to the Rambla building. I can remember being slightly disappointed whenever I went into this shop, as the name evoked expectations of cream cakes, sticky buns and other goodies. However, as I recall, it mainly sold vegetables and flowers, with only a few sweets on display. Miss Thew was the proprietor, and I may be wrong but I think there was some connection with the East Yorkshire Motor Services, as I can remember often seeing the bus drivers and conductors meeting there. Perhaps there was a cup of tea or coffee to be had there?

The Market Place was a major passenger collection point for EYMS, whose dark blue and yellow buses would be seen coming from and going to Hull, Bridlington, Scarborough, York, and all the surrounding villages. The Town Service buses also ran from the Market Place. These were run by Mr. Cherry, whose garage was in Queensgate, and were single-decked cream-coloured buses which provided a local service in Beverley. Cherry's Coaches also ran seaside and mystery trips at weekends. These usually departed from the Market Place, and were very popular. The centre of the Market Place was marked by a row of four telephone boxes, with wooden seats to the front, which were much used by waiting bus passengers.

There were two ironmongers' shops in the Market Place that I can recall. One, of course, is Briggs and Powell, which is still flourishing today, although I do not think it sold many electrical goods in those early days. Mr. Kitson and Mr. Jones were two of the managers . The other ironmonger's was to be found across the Market Place, occupying the corner where Lloyds Bank is today. I think that this shop was called Morris's, and I do remember that you could see pots and pans hanging outside the shop, and brushes and bass brooms were displayed on the pavement. Next door to Morris the ironmonger was a small café called Rutherford's, which by the late Fifties and early Sixties became a café-cum-coffee bar called Haversnack, which was run by Mr. Roy Francis, who had been a well-known rugby league player.

I can remember the Globe Inn was just in Ladygate, at the north-eastern corner of the Market Place. There always seemed to be caravans and horses tethered in the yard just through the archway that made up the frontage of the Inn. I never went into the yard, but I think perhaps the Globe may have been popular with travellers. Mr. Harry Tomlinson, watchmaker and jeweller, had his shop at the top end of the Market Place, beneath the clock. I well recall taking my clockwork train to Mr. Tomlinson many times to repair broken springs due to over-winding. I think the business is still in the same family as it is very much unchanged. Names that spring to mind when recalling that area are Skingle's, who I think were drapers, Irene Bloom, a ladies' fashion shop, Laughton's the butchers, and Meadow the grocer. Kemps Corner was at the northern end of the Market Place, at its junction with Lairgate and North Bar Within, and it was here that Mr. Simson had what I think was the only pet shop in Beverley. I have distant memories of a grey parrot being one of the attractions there. Mr. Simson became a mayor of Beverley.

I cannot recall any building societies having premises in the Market Place in those days. The local society, the Beverley Building Society, was tucked away in a small office in Lairgate opposite Briggs and Powell's passage. I think Mr. Richardson was the manager in those days. I can remember one of my errands was to go there to 'pay building'. However, I slightly digress. Back to the Market Place where I was to remember the banks. The Yorkshire Penny Bank was located between Burton's and the King's Head. This bank had a children's account organised and operated by the infant schools. I can remember having a little blue bankbook contained in a cloth bag with drawstrings that one took to school each week with your penny, or pennies. This bank is now known as the Yorkshire Bank. There was the York County Savings Bank, which is now the TSB. Mr. Metcalfe was one of the managers. Actually I still have an account with the York County with 6s. 7d. in it. Lloyds Bank I think was located close to where the Globe Inn used to be. The Westminster Bank became the NatWest, after merging with the National Provincial, and I think the Midland Bank was always the Midland and located where it is today, although a name change has just taken place.

Other retail establishments in the Market Place were Dove's fish and chip shop, Drewery's china shop, Malin's the drapers, Argenta the butchers, Laughton's the greengrocers, Brusby's estate

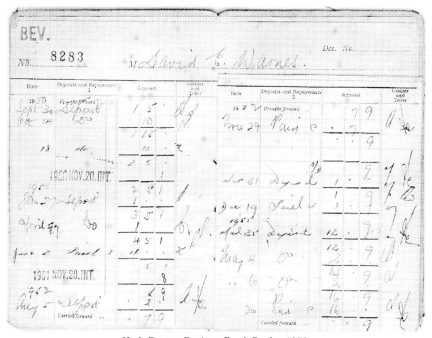

York County Savings Bank Book c.1950.

agents, Ellarby's turf accountant's, which was just down Dyer Lane, Gee's wet fish shop, Tiplady's baby and children's outfitters, the same family having a pork butcher's, also in the Market Place. Then there was Green's the stationers, who I think had links with the local newspaper, the *Beverley Guardian*. Green's also sold quality glassware and china. I remember that one of the ladies who worked at Green's was Mrs. Jackson, whose husband, Mr. Kenneth Jackson, became a mayor of Beverley. There was the well-established furniture store of William Hutchinson, and also Brown's the tailors, and Medici the jeweller. Stead and Simpson had their other shop on the corner of Old Waste, and Field's Café was just opposite the Market Cross. There will, I know, be some omissions, and perhaps at a later time more recollections of other businesses will come to mind. However, Saturday Market was just as its name suggests, a market held on a Saturday, and it has not changed in that respect, only the stallholders and to some extent the produce has changed. I can remember Mr. Ocky Clark's vegetable stall, with his sister supervising operations, and Mr. Sellers' vegetable and flower stall. Then I can recall a gentleman selling boots and shoes whose well-known shout was 'No obligation to buy'. One of Burgess's icecream vans was always to be found there on market day selling their renowned icecream. They are still there today, one of the few unchanging aspects of the town market. A really well-known Beverley character was Nixie Oliver, who was always to be found in the Market Place selling his newspapers. He would stand in all weathers, with his paperbag slung in front of him, and I believe that he continued his service, despite infirmity, well into old age. I can recall, too, the local hauliers Mr. Roy Brusby, and Mr. Peter Haddlesey, with their horses and carts being in attendance on market days.

Fairs seemed to be frequently held in Saturday Market, with many rides and sideshows to be enjoyed. When the fairs came to town, they were held in the widest part of the Market Place, and the regular weekend traders would move down to the Market Cross end. I can remember such rides as the Helter Skelter, and Noah's Ark, Bumper Cars and Chairoplanes all whizzing around to the popular songs of the time. One that I for some reason particularly remember was *My Truly, Truly Fair*. I think it was sung by Guy Mitchell, although I cannot be sure. I would marvel at the skill of the showmen as they took the fares whilst the rides were in full motion. Among the sideshows were coconut shies, rifle ranges, and

*Saturday
Market Stalls.
c.1953.*

Trading in Saturday Market c.1953.

darts. It was always difficult to win a prize. The most common prize seemed to be pot Alsatian dogs, which were a fashion of the time, and could be seen displayed in some front room windows. I always enjoyed the fairs.

On certain days of the year the Market Place was used for military parades. The town had the East Yorkshire Regiment's barracks in Victoria Road, and at Leconfield an operational Royal Air Force station. I can recall a military band playing in the Market Place led by the bandmaster, Mr. Purcell. I think that this was the East Yorkshire Regimental Band. The Beverley Church Lads Brigade band would often lead parades in the Market Place too.

When Beverley Races were held, the Market Place was always busy. Full of race-going people, there was almost a carnival feel about the place. Touts, tipsters and I am sure a few unsavoury characters were all there, as there were always two or three policemen about. I can remember seeing escapologists performing, and the cheers as they would writhe and wriggle free from canvas bags wrapped around with heavy chains and padlocks. I had the good fortune to see, on one such day, the famous racing tipster, Ras Prince Monolulu. He was a tall black gentleman, who wore a Zulu head dress, and sold racing tips. His catch-phrase was 'I gotta horse'. I knew who it was as I identified him from his portrait on a cigarette card.

CHAPTER THREE

Streets off the Town Centre

Lairgate is a long street, running from Keldgate to North Bar Within. Starting then from the Keldgate end, I can recall Mr. Baker's cycle repair shop was opposite a fish and chip shop, Granville's I think it was. They fried using coal, which I am sure resulted in a tastier product. The old Beehive public house was just further along. I was always intrigued by the actual old-fashioned beehive that was the inn sign. Opposite the public house I remember Chick Verity's rag, bone, and scrap yard. I cannot remember Mr. Verity as I think that Mr. Reg Wilson was the owner in my day, although everybody still seemed to call it Chick Verity's. A short distance from there was the Tiger Inn, which I think sold Darley's Ales, and opposite was a flower shop and nursery run by Mr. Sellers. The small green not far from the public house was used by us young lads to play football and cricket. This was not always approved of, and we would often be chased away by a very cross lady whose house bordered the green. Hebb's motor garage was opposite the green, and I may be wrong but I think that Mrs. Hebb – or was it Miss Hebb? – had musical connections. Next to Hebb's was the entrance to a small local industry, William Stephenson, the coachbuilder. My father was employed there as a craftsman for some years.

The Hall, the former office of Beverley Corporation, still stands in its grounds in Lairgate today, although no longer in use. Beverley Corporation sadly exists no longer, and this lovely old building has been sold. I can recall that one of my errands as a boy was to take the rates money to the Hall, and have it counted and checked by Mr. Rispin. Mr. Ernest Bailey was the Town Clerk and I can remember him wearing his wig and gown when parading with local dignitaries in the town. Another boyhood memory is of collecting beechnuts from the big beech trees that stood in the grounds, on the way home from school. There was a room in the Hall decorated with some very expensive Chinese wallpaper which was the subject of some controversy concerning its cost. I wonder if it is still there, and what will become of it? What is now the Memorial Hall was in those days the disused church of St. John, which, we used to think, might be haunted, but this is probably because it looked very forbidding in its dilapidation. Nevertheless, we used to play around the old church, but always in the daylight. In those days there was even a Beverley Rural District Council. I remember it had its headquarters in Lairgate, just past the Champney Road junction.

Just opposite Landress Lane were some large Georgian town houses, the offices of E. W. Wells, who I think had something to do with the timber trade. I remember these houses well, as a family friend, Mrs. Dorothy Griffiths, and her daughter, Jeanette, lived in a flat at the very top of the buildings. Much fun was to be had exploring these huge houses, and family visits there were always eagerly anticipated. I well recall one November 5th, when a firework display was organised in the garden, which incidentally contained a large air raid shelter. A stray spark ignited the large box of fireworks, and they all went off together. Nobody was hurt, the air raid shelter was not needed, but it was a good display of very short duration, received with much good humour, which was a characteristic of Mrs. Griffiths. Much of that garden is now a car park.

I can remember Mr. Bielby's wet fish and game shop, just next to the Windmill public house. There would always be an impressive seasonal display of pheasants, partridges, hares, wood-pigeons and rabbits hung around the shop. Other businesses in Lairgate were Mr. Worsfold, the barber, who was just opposite the rear of Hutchinson's furniture store, and Mr. Skinner's fish and chip shop which was where the current fish and chip shop is. Skinner's were well-known for quality. Mrs. Dilcock I can remember was frying and serving. Somewhere in that run of buildings I can remember a building that was the headquarters of the local Girl Guides. I am sure I used to go to parties there when I was in the Scouts. Further along, as mentioned before, were the offices of the Beverley Building Society, and then a saddler's business. This shop had a life-size replica of a horse's head in the window, and was owned by Mr. Skinner, who I do not think was a relative of the fish and chip shop proprietor. Next came Rutherford's fruit and vegetable shop, which was always very busy. I think perhaps that they had some connection with the café in the Market Place. Next to the Cross Keys Hotel, which sold Hammond's Ales, there was Mr. Harry Robert's pork shop, renowned far and wide for its pork pies, sausages and other pork products. There would always be queues most Friday and Saturday mornings. Mr. Roberts was a mayor of Beverley. Finally, I remember that the coal merchant's, Good, Havercroft, had their offices just along from Mr. Robert's shop.

Down Ladygate, just off the Market Place, were the Beverley

Swimming Baths. This was probably one of the smallest public swimming baths in the country, and we used to go there for swimming lessons from Miss Phyllis Capstick, who was a well-known local competitive swimmer. I must confess that as far as she was concerned I was no water baby. It seemed to take me all my time to stay afloat. Mr. Mendham, I recall, saw to the efficient running of the baths. Also down Ladygate was the headquarters of one of the local Boy Scout troops. I cannot remember which troop it was, but I recall the meetings of all the Beverley Scout troops at the Ladygate HQ prior to the Armistice Day parades. Mr. Braithwaite's lodging house was just across Dog and Duck Lane opposite the public house of the same name. At the rear of the Baths, a small passage ran through to the Market Place where Mr. Akrill of the gunshop had a bicycle showroom. I was told that long ago this passage was known as the Fish Shambles.

There was only one Walkergate in those days, no Old and New as there is today. I can well remember Mrs. Taylor's general store next to the infants' school at the northern end of Walkergate. It was one of those shops which was open all hours, and sold almost everything. If Mrs. Taylor wasn't on hand to serve you, then her son Eric was. He was a rather portly gentleman, often to be seen making deliveries around the town on his bicycle. Walkergate House, I think, had something to do with the Government, probably National Insurance. Another shop, almost opposite Walkergate House, was 'Nacky' Norris's hardware store. Mr. Norris always had a selection of brushes and shovels on display outside the shop. We always bought our Bonfire Night fireworks from him. Spencer School, a small primary school, was just off Walkergate. Every year on a certain day the pupils would be given free oranges, which I think was a long-standing tradition. I didn't go to Spencer School, but I thought it was a good tradition. It is now a car park.

Lord Roberts Road and Champney Road both hold special memories. The Beverley School Clinic was down Lord Roberts Road. I well recall my visits there as a small child for health checks. There was a playroom with a beautiful rocking horse, and other toys to take a small child's mind away from the job in hand. They would give out the Government-issue orange juice at the clinic. This came in a flat glass bottle with a screw cap. It had a unique flavour that I have not come across since. I did have occasion to visit the clinic as a patient when, as a small boy, I and some other small boys contracted impetigo, a skin disease resulting in erupting spots appearing in various places, but mostly on the face. It was cured by applying Gentian Violet to the affected parts. The trouble was that every one knew you had impetigo because of the blue blotches where the Gentian Violet had been applied, so for a short while one was akin to being a leper. There was a countrywide polio epidemic in the Fifties, and everyone received their sugar lump vaccine at the clinic. Another fact about the Beverley School Clinic was that during the war, when all place names were removed to confuse the enemy, the letters of the word Beverley were removed, leaving just the words School Clinic. However, the removal of the letters still left the word Beverley stencilled in the grime of the stonework, and thus was Beverley identified to any enemy, then and many years after the war and even up to the time of writing. Opposite the clinic, and on the corner of Well Lane, was a large wooden hut type of building. I think it was the YMCA or some similar organisation; perhaps the St. John Ambulance Brigade used it too.

Beverley Public Library in Champney Road holds many memories. Just outside the main entrance was a wooden, glass fronted cabinet which housed barometers, thermometers, and hygrometers. Daily weather records were kept and displayed there. It was an interesting and a quite unique facility, which sadly is no longer there. Mr. Whiteley was the Chief Librarian and I joined this library at the earliest opportunity. I remember my application form for the children's section being scrutinised by Mrs. Braithwaite, who was in charge of such things, and was as I recall very well organised. The building housed a museum at the top of the grand staircase. I often wonder what happened to the collection of exhibits, which included a room full of stuffed animals and birds. I well recall leopards, foxes, and many species of wild bird. Yes, it was a sort of natural history room, and it was of great interest to me. I know that the huge oil painting at the head of the gallery depicting a stampede of cattle will always be remembered, the sense of panic in the herd was so very real, and it is no less impressive now. I was always stirred by this painting and hope that it is being cared for and allowed to hang there for many years to come. The impressive staircase to the Art Gallery also had grand bannisters, which we young lads would never lose an opportunity to slide down – that was providing that Mrs. Braithwaite wasn't around. Also in Champney Road, between Lord Roberts Road and Princes Gardens, was a little sweet shop. I can remember buying liquorice root and cinnamon sticks there, but I cannot recall who owned it

Well Lane was where Mr. Yengo Benson lived. He was a well-known local boxer, and I can recall seeing him about the town, although I never saw him fight. My memory of him is tinged with sadness as I knew his son Roy, who was at Minster Infants School in the same class as me. Roy died during his time at the school, and I remember all of us children being told, and the collection we made for a floral tribute. It was a sorrowful moment. I can recall a large yard in Well Lane with some caravans which I know were occupied at the time. That area is now the rear of Boyes department store. Dr. Nye's house and surgery were on the corner of Cross Street and Well Lane, next to the East Riding of Yorkshire Council garage, with the County Hall buildings just opposite occupying a much smaller site than they do today. My uncle, Mr. Sam Shaw, was employed at the County Council garage, and also Mr. Fred Waddington worked there too. Register Square I thought was never really a square, more just a sort of L-shaped street. Beverley's main Post Office is still situated there. My Grandad Warnes was a postman there until his retirement in 1936, about a year before I was born. Opposite the Post Office the County Council had a Licensing Office where we would go to renew Road Fund and Driving Licences. Mr. Gordon Cumins worked there and dealt with all the renewals. Just around the corner was the Guildhall, which incorporated the Mayor's Parlour, the Council Chamber and Magistrates' and Coroner's Courts. I can recall that Mrs. Gow and Mr. Hawkins were magistrates, although I fortunately never saw them in their official capacity. Next came the Beverley Police Station, which was the main office of the Beverley Division of the East Riding Constabulary. Three much respected and popular officers of the time, I remember well, were Pc Lucius Holmes, Pc Bill Coverdale, and Sgt Brenda Ushaw, who were often to be seen patrolling the streets of Beverley. Next to the Licensing Office the local Constabulary had a billiard and snooker room, in what was long ago called Holland House, when it was a small private school. The full-size snooker table was really too large for the room, but this was overcome by the provision of a much shortened cue for certain shots.

North Bar Within was the beginning of what I perceived to be the 'posh end of the town'. Taking the eastern side first, I think that it was Miss Nicholl's ladies' fashion shop just before Barclay's Bank. I can remember Mr. Phil Ellerington, a well-known local cricketer, was a cashier at Barclay's. Along from the bank and passing the Beaver public house and an estate agent's was Mr.

Tom Hollingsworth's photographic shop and studio. Mr. Hollingsworth was well-known for a particularly outstanding photograph of Beverley Minster which was used in magazines and on picture postcards. Next was Mr. Holmes's papershop. Occasionally one of my errands was to call there to pick up a copy of the *Nursing Mirror* for my aunt, who was a matron at a hospital in Ilkley. This errand was always a puzzle to me because the periodical was ordered in the name of a mysterious Sister Harbord, and not in my aunt's name. I never did find out who Sister Harbord was. As far as the *Nursing Mirror* was concerned I have to confess that I succumbed to curiosity and read bits of it on the way home. This I think was the reason for passing bouts of hypochondria which afflicted me at the time. Snowy Hall, the greengrocer, was next, on the corner of Hengate. I remember him as a small gentleman with spectacles and a trilby hat. When Mr. Hall retired, the shop became an electrical store owned by my uncle, Mr. Arthur Wilson. It was called Beavercraft.

Going on then past St. Mary's church, where I had a brief flirtation with bell ringing [I think that Mr. Braithwaite was in charge], we come to St. Mary's Manor which during the war and for some years afterwards was known as 'War Ag'. Then it became an office for the Ministry of Agriculture, and later it was filled with agronomists and agricultural advisers and known as East Riding ADAS. It has recently been sold I think to a property company. I have a thought that the passage down the north side of the Manor led to some racing stables, as there were two or three racehorse trainers in the town. It may have been Billy Hammet's, but I'm not sure. I can recall overhearing a conversation in one of the local hostelries concerning one of Billy Hammet's horses that had apparently taken a stable lad in its mouth, and then 'shook 'im like a varmint'. I do not know if this was true or not, but I have never forgotten it. Next was Mr. Scruton's florist's. Mr. Scruton was mayor of Beverley on more than one occasion. Then, just next to the Royal Standard public house, was, and still is today, Burgess's ice cream shop. It was not such a large enterprise in those days, but it was known for its quality locally, and is now to be found countrywide. Mr. Mark Burgess, the owner, was also a mayor of Beverley, and I can recall that his son, Ian, was an accomplished singer.

Going back to where North Bar Within joins Lairgate, and opposite Barclay's Bank, I can recall Mr. Dunning's salerooms. I think auction sales were held there every week, with furniture and other household items going under the hammer. Messrs. Brusby and Haddlesey would be on hand to transport goods to and from the sale. Abram's café was close by the salerooms, and I remember the aroma of freshly made coffee emanating from the interior. Mr. Annison, the chemist, was next, followed by a barber's shop named Savoy. There was a fishmonger next, by the name of Botham. I can remember Mr. Jebson, the butcher, was just opposite St. Mary's church, and just before the Beverley Arms. I can recall waiting in a large crowd outside the Beverley Arms to see Wilfred Pickles arrive after *Have A Go* had been held at the new Longcroft School. He was, as I remember, very late arriving, and I suffered some chastisement and an embarrassing moment when I returned home at a very late hour. I did not see either Mabel or Barney.

Arnott's Cake shop was to be found just after the Beverley Arms. It also incorporated a popular tea shop and café. Next came a shop selling electrical goods, which belonged to Mr. Hales, and this was followed by a quality furniture store called Hasslewood Taylor's. I can well recall Gordon Armstrong's garage, which occupied all the old Tudor building on the corner of Tiger Lane. Armstrong's garage extended well down Tiger Lane. I can remember the petrol pumps at the entrance to the garage. These pumps had extended supply pipes which swung across the pavement at a height which allowed pedestrians to walk underneath. Self-service was unheard of then. Just after the garage was an old disused cemetery, formerly attached to St. Mary's I think. This site was chosen to be a garden to commemorate the coronation of Queen Elizabeth II.

Coming now into Hengate, D. J. Bromby's, then the only sports shop in Beverley, was to be found. It was owned by Mr. Jack Bromby, and was a magic place for a sports-mad young boy. Every sport seemed to be catered for, and the window displays at the start of each different sporting season were spellbinding. Bromby's, which also sold suitcases, briefcases and the like has closed relatively recently, and is now boarded-up awaiting who knows what. Perhaps yet another 'fashionable' restaurant. I mourn its passing. Leak's brush works were situated just along from the Ladygate junction. I recall that Mr. Tom Leak was a mayor of Beverley. I remember Arden's Vaults in Hengate selling wine, and next, of course, the famous White Horse public house, which successive landlords have, to their credit, endeavoured to preserve as it was when the Collinson family ran it. I first went into the White Horse as a very young man with one of my uncles, and remember sitting in the gentlemen's bar on shiny leather seats stuffed with horse hair. Miss Nellie Collinson, a slim, darkly dressed, almost birdlike little lady, or her sister, Miss Dorothy, who was rather larger, with, I always thought, an air of serenity about her, would serve the customers, as their brother, Tim, would see to the gas lighting, fires and such things. As young men we would spend many a Saturday night in the White Horse, before going on to some of the other attractions in the town. The Collinsons kept the place spotless. All the tables and the stone floors were always scrubbed clean, and even then, when they were elderly, I cannot recall anything but an orderly well-run establishment with a warm and welcoming touch to it. The Old Ale they sold was very popular, and also very potent.

Now to Norwood, and the first building on the corner of Manor Road was the recently demolished Regal Cinema and Ballroom. This quite modern building housed a cinema, the largest of the three in Beverley at that time, a café and a large ballroom. When popular films were being shown I can remember queues forming in the large foyer. The cinema section ran a children's Saturday morning film show, and the children attending were known as the ABC Minors. It was run in a more organised way than the Marble Arch children's filmshows: in that one had to fill in a form and get a badge to become an ABC Minor, and I can recall it involved children from the audience being called on to the stage to take part in games, run by a lady known to the kids as 'Aunty Nandy'. Led by her, we all had to sing *We are the Minors of the ABC* to, I think, one of the Sousa march tunes before each show. The shows cost 6d., and I have to say that many of us preferred the Marble Arch shows at half the price and with less organisation. The manager of the cinema at the time was a gentleman called Archie. I cannot remember his surname.

The Regal Ballroom held many very special memories for me. In our late teenage years to our early twenties we would be found there most Saturday nights dancing the night away to the music of Harry Chatterton and his Band. The format was much the same every Saturday night, starting at the White Horse, or for some the Valiant Soldier, and then to the dance. Quicksteps, foxtrots and modern waltzes would follow each other in quick succession with always the *Gay Gordons* in there somewhere. As the night progressed there would be 'Ladies Excuse Me' quicksteps, the *Palais Glide* and the *Hokey Cokey*, but for many of us the Last

The Mayor, Coun. P. D. Dunn, inspecting a regimental guard of honour outside the Regal cinema. c.1953.

Waltz was the crowning moment, when one's expectations and hopes were either realised or shattered. Still, one could be certain that there would always be another Saturday night. Harry Chatterton's band consisted of about 12 accomplished musicians and was very much in demand locally. I remember them dressed in their blue jackets, black trousers and bow ties, playing the popular tunes of the day very professionally. The lady singer attached to the band was a lovely blonde lady called Sheila, who would sit on stage awaiting her turn to sing. She would mostly sing the romantic ballads of the moment, something, say, in the style of Ruby Murray with her song, *Softly Softly,* or perhaps in the style of Joan Regan, as they were both very popular at the time. The band also had a very skilful drummer, and most dance nights he would do a solo turn to the music, *Skin Deep.* This would bring the dancing to a standstill as everyone in the room crowded to the front of the stage to watch and applaud his frantic performance. There was an interval halfway through the night to allow the band a break, when it was possible to attend the bar or obtain a 'passout', which allowed you to go to the White Horse or the Valiant Soldier. I cannot leave the Regal Ballroom without mentioning the resident Master of Ceremonies, Mr. Bert Baker. A tall man of military bearing, always smartly dressed in dinner jacket, black bow tie, etc., with his swept-

Publicity displays for films at the Regal cinema. c.1955.

back curly silver hair and his neat moustache, Bert Baker had a dignified authority which commanded respect. I am sure there would be some occasions when his authority was needed to restore order but I cannot personally recall any. So now the Regal with its cinema and ballroom is gone, and the whys and wherefores of its demise I am sure have been debated by many, but I just feel a certain sadness that such an asset is no more. Passing through the bingo stage, the snooker stage, and finally the ultimate indignity of neglect followed by demolition, this once fine building will endure in the memories of all those young people of Beverley and the surrounding villages, who, passing through its doors, danced so many nights away.

Across from the Regal and next to Healey's the butchers was an agricultural merchants called Collison. This site eventually became the Clock Service Garage, which has only recently closed down. Mr. Derek Ellerington was one of the proprietors. On the site now occupied by Safeways there was Massey's garage and car showroom. The agricultural merchant's, the Holderness Plough Company, was just along the road. Further up Norwood is the entrance to the cattle market, which, as I write, is under threat of closure or re-siting. This market traded on Mondays for fat stock cattle and on Wednesdays, which was always the main trading day, for store stock cattle. In those days it was a very hive of activity with auctions of poultry, sheep, pigs, cattle and goats all taking place. It was a weekly meeting place for the local farmers and other agricultural people, where topics such as the weather, land conditions, and the price of corn would be earnestly discussed. Modern times, I am sure, have reduced the importance of this venue, but it is hoped that it can be saved in its present position. Just at the side of the cattle market, on what is now the Morton Lane car park was the Beverley Labour Exchange. Also in Norwood I recall that Mr. Victor Millet lived in one of a pair of fine houses almost opposite the Wellington Road junction. Mr. Millet was a Beverley character who dealt in works of art. I remember the house, as one of the Minster curates, the Rev. Donald Fehrenbach, lived there for a while, and took confirmation classes. I seem to recall that he went on to a high office within the Church of England. Norwood Recreation Ground was where the local schools had their sports days. My athletic debut, representing Minster Boys School, ended ignominiously when one of my borrowed spiked shoes came off during my first race.

North Bar Without and New Walk in those days really was, to

Cattle Market scenes. c.1953.

us youngsters, the 'posh' end of town. When I was a Boy Scout that area was the place to be during 'Bob a Job' week, and proceeds from the smallest task would always be at least a florin or even half a crown. Just through the North Bar on the corner of York Road there is the Rose and Crown public house. Mr. Leach was the landlord in those days. The beer served was Darley's, and there was a room in the pub reserved for gentlemen only, where some of Beverley's professional people could be found at lunch times. I think that upstairs was a billiard room, but I never played there. Wylies Road was not a thoroughfare in those days, merely an alley leading through to Manor Road, emerging opposite the entrance to another well-known Beverley enterprise, Watts Brothers' transport. The side of this alleyway was overgrown with elder bushes and therefore a good adventure area for children. Beverley Conservative Club was much smaller than it is now and I think that it fronted onto North Bar Without before the major Wylies Road alterations.

Next to the Conservative Club was the residence and studio of Mr. Sandy Lewis, a very well-known local photographer. Mr. Lewis, who was confined to a wheelchair following a childhood bout of polio, was famous locally for his portrait and wedding photography. One of his famous sitters was the comedian, George Formby, who I think must have had a horse under training at one of the local stables, as his portrait was taken in full riding gear. Just prior to my leaving school I had the privilege of working for Mr. Lewis, and I was entrusted with quite a few wedding assignments on his behalf. Sometimes on very busy Saturdays I would photograph two or three weddings. Another young man called Rodney also assisted with the weddings. I can remember that Miss Hazel Drew worked at the studio as an assistant to Mr. Lewis in his studio and processing work. Sadly the studio is no longer there, and I often wonder what happened to the people whose weddings I photographed. It was happy work, and I hope they were happy too.

I remember Harper's garage was just along the road. In fact, Mr. Lewis used to keep his car there, as towards the rear of the main workshop were some rented garages belonging to Mr. Harper. Mr. Lewis had a lovely old Lanchester with hand controls which I was allowed to reverse out of the garage for him. Across from Harper's garage is Peel Place, at the far end of which was Mr. Denis Dunn's veterinary practice. Mr. Dunn became a mayor of Beverley. Next is a terrace of large houses. In one of these Mr. Beddoes, the dentist, had his practice. Fortunately my visits to Mr. Beddoes were limited but unforgettable, probably for both of us, as I know that I was not the best of patients. The practice later I can recall belonged to Mr. Coates. Further along and set well back was a large Georgian house where our family doctor practised. Firstly, when I was very young it was Dr. Scott, who died whilst still in practice, and he was followed by Dr. Edwin Baker, who was our family doctor for many years until his retirement. I think that Dr. Baker was involved with the St. John Ambulance Brigade.

The Sessions House in New Walk holds many special personal memories, for that was the site of my very first job after leaving school at the age of nearly 17. As well as being a Court House, where the County Quarter Sessions were held, the Sessions House was also the headquarters of the East Riding Constabulary, a force to which I was appointed as a police cadet, attached to the CID. In those days there were very few exemptions to National Service, and being employed as a police cadet was not one of them. However, for nearly 18 months that was to be my role, and very memorable it was too. Although after my National Service I did not return to police work, the changes that took place did not escape my notice, and when the ill-conceived County of Humberside was born my thoughts often returned to that well respected and efficient local police force, the East Riding Constabulary, which was to be lost forever.

The Chief Constable in those long gone days was Mr. J. W. P. Blenkin, and his deputy was Mr. Bowler. The Chief Constable's office was on the top floor of the Sessions House, and, as the CID was on the ground floor, I did not see him very often, although I was, on the occasion of a visit by HM Inspector of Constabularies, called upon to meet his official car as it arrived at the Sessions House, open the door, and smartly salute him as he alighted with the Inspector. The CID was a very busy department, and as well as being an active crime detection unit it embraced a records department, an Information Room where all day-to-day intelligence was assessed and actioned, a Radio Control Room, to which all the patrol cars reported, and a Photographic Section. The telephone communications system for the force was also housed within the CID. The first police patrol cars used [and that was about four years before my employment] were small black two-seater MG sports cars. During my short time with the force they were Austin Somersets, and Ford Zephyrs, and they were always painted black. The role of the police cadet, when not making cups of tea or washing up, was to keep records up to date, man the radio [call sign M2XT], the switchboard, and type reports 'phoned in by beat constables. There were also occasions when I had to help out with Police Dog training. At that time the force had two dogs, Pluto, a Dobermann Pinscher, and Quantur, an Alsatian. John Martin and Cliff Beacock were their handlers. The training went something like this. We would all get in the black Jowett dog van and go on to the Westwood. I would then be instructed to run off into the bushes and after a few minutes the dogs would be released to track me down. I was advised to find a climbable tree as quickly as possible, which luckily I always did. However, I did enjoy the work with the dogs. The

East Riding Constabulary ran a football team, which, using Hodgson's recreation ground as their home pitch, played in the local Thursday League, against such teams as RAF Patrington, and Fish Bobbers. It was a good way to spend a Thursday afternoon, and I always enjoyed playing.

The Sessions House now is as far as I can see just another Police Station, being part of the Humberside force. I do not think that it is a major criminal court now, so it is much changed, although I am sure it still plays an important part in policing matters. Many of the people, both policemen and civilians whom I worked for and with during my short stay, were most helpful to a youngster just out of school, and I will always remember them with affection and gratitude. Looking back, they were indeed a dedicated group, and, with hindsight, had not other opportunities arisen, I dare say I would have happily settled for a policeman's lot after my National Service. The following people I can well recall: Dennis Beal, Jack Burton, Leslie Cooper, Mrs. Ellenton, Bernard Gray, Tom Henigan, Norman Henson, Ron Jennison, John Simpson, David Oliver, Jack Forth, Ian Brocklesby, Eric Carver, John Shillito, Ray Langdale, Fred Evans, Richard Hall, Peter Judd, Charlie Groce, Jock Dempster, Cornelius Boam, Jock Wilkinson, Tom Higgins, Barry Peacock, Ken Dale, Len Straker, Don Foster, Paul Berriman, Owen Sykes-Bundy, Harry Walker-Smith and Millicent Megson. They were all part of my life at the time, and all played their part in the effective and much respected East Riding Constabulary.

There are some other memories of New Walk, the first being the convent, which was situated in Norfolk Street, just behind the Sessions House, and another was the little shop across the road just next to St. Mary's cemetery. This was Miss Backhouse's, and it sold groceries and general provisions. I think that this little business also had a nursery at the rear which provided flowers and plants for the shop. As far as the convent was concerned, it just seemed to me that the nuns quietly and unobtrusively went about their devotions, and I cannot recall any real contact with them during my time at the Sessions House, apart from seeing them in passing. Gallows Lane, which is just opposite St. Mary's cemetery, led to a hospital where wounded servicemen from the war were treated. This building was then used for some years as temporary accommodation for St. Mary's Boys primary school, after the school buildings in Mill Lane were burned down in the late Forties. The site is now Beverley College.

Country
dancing at St.
Mary's Boys
School
[Longcroft Hall]
c.1954.

CHAPTER FOUR

Closer again to home

Having recalled Highgate in an earlier chapter, I mention it again as it leads to the Collegiate and Parish Church of Beverley Minster, which, along with its immediate area, holds so many personal memories. The first 25 years of my life were spent, not as some would say in the shadow of the Minster, but rather in its light, although in those early years that was only a partial realisation, and it is in the recollections that one has later in life that appreciation truly dawns. Beverley Minster remains unchanged. It is only in its surroundings and inevitably in its people that I have seen the major changes. This chapter, then, remembers the Minster, and its surroundings as they were for me in my boyhood.

I was christened in the Minster, although, of course, I do not recall it, but I do remember joining the Choir. I would be about nine or ten years old when I was accepted as a probationer. Probationers sat at the rear of the choirstalls and wore just the red cassock, without the white surplice and ruff. Before long I

Beverley Minster. View from Long Lane. c.1952

View from the north tower of the Minster. The Girls' School, the Parish Room, Vicarage and garden can be plainly identified. Mr. Long's SS Jaguar can also be seen. c.1954.

became a fully fledged chorister, and was placed on the Cantoris side. The Minster Organist and Choirmaster at that time was Mr. John Long, who was a lovely man and an accomplished musician and whose patience at times I'm sure I sorely tried. Practices were held on weekday mornings before school, and on two evenings a week before evensong, as well as after Sunday morning services. If at times my attention wandered or I sang off key, usually flatly, I was brought back to concentration by a well aimed *Songs of Praise*. Eventually, having gained a medal from the Royal School of Church Music, I became one of the senior choirboys and remained with the Choir until nature took its course. The Choir sometimes would go on trips to York Minster to sing with other choirs. I remember that Dr. Francis Jackson was the Organist and Choirmaster there. These trips were memorable as they usually involved a journey by steam train, direct from Beverley to York in those days, and a day out in York, going around the museums. Once when only five boys were needed we all travelled in Mr. Long's red MG sports car. Mr. Long always had classic cars. I remember well his cream SS Jaguar, a beautiful car.

Although I did not appreciate it then, being a member of the Minster Choir was such a privilege, and it was only much later in life that it became clear just how special those years in the Choir were. Many of the hymns, the psalms, responses, settings and the anthems are still with me today. The joyful *Te Deums,* the *Benedicite, Venite* and the *Magnificats,* and the solemn *Nunc Dimittis,* yes, I can recall them all. Certain anthems also remain with me. One of my favourites was *Beati Quorum,* and another was *Ave Verum Corpus,* but there were so many beautiful pieces, indeed too many to mention here. Christmas is remembered for the bass solo of Arnold Bennett in *Three Kings from Persian Lands Afar,* and Harvest Festival for the tenor of Tom Lewis in *Thou Visitest the Earth.* I remember too the alto voice of Leslie Giles in the plaintive *This is the Record of John.* On Easter Sundays, at nine o'clock in the morning, the choir would climb the steps of the north tower and sing the hymn *Jesus Christ is risen today* from the top of the tower. Still breathless from the climb, we sang our hearts out up there. Times in the choir are remembered too for human moments, for instance, when one of the senior choirmen, Mr. Jack Acaster, would pass his tin of liquorice 'nippets' round during the Vicar's sermon, or, when my voice was breaking and I was unable to sing, Mr. Long would place pieces of paper on the organ keys, and go down from the organ loft to conduct the choir, leaving me waiting for his signal to play the chord marked by the paper to start the unaccompanied anthem. If ever just one of those pieces of paper had moved I dread to think what the consequences would have been. Choristers remembered are Norman Wilson, Michael Dunning, David Sleight, Tom Barker, Stephen and Clive Turgoose, Michael Haley, Garry Craggs, Sidney Mawer, Michael Griggs, Nicholas Long, and the two Pearson brothers. I did not realise it at the time, but those few short years of service gave me a love of music and singing that has lasted a lifetime. I am deeply grateful.

The first Vicar that I can remember at the Minster was the Rev. D. T. Dick. He must have either retired or moved to another parish, for he was succeeded by the Rev. Colwyn Hargreaves who was to be the incumbent Vicar of the Minster during all the years of my choir membership and for some time afterwards. He was a gentle and kindly man as I recall, who had I think seen service with the Royal Navy during the war. He used to wear a duffle coat when not on duty, and this in those days was quite rare and served to confirm to us youngsters that he had indeed seen service at sea. Mrs. Hargreaves and their three daughters were involved in the activities of the parish. I can remember them as being a popular family. Other people who were directly involved in the church were Mr. Pateman, who was the verger; he was followed in that position by Mr. Eric Milner. Sidesmen and church officials of the day were Mr. Witty, Mr. Whitelam, Mr. Proctor, Mr. Tanfield, Mr. Forster and Miss Gliddon. Mr. Barker was in charge of the bell ringing. One of my uncles, the late Mr. Laurie Parker, was a bellringer at the Minster, and also an official guide to visitors. Somewhat of an amateur local historian and archaeologist, his knowledge of Beverley Minster was vast, and he recorded much of the research that he carried out. Unfortunately those records cannot be found today among the personal effects that he left, but I was shown them as a young man so I know that they did exist, and I can only hope that they are safe somewhere.

Minster Yard North was where, as choirboys, we would play football while waiting for choir practice to commence. This always annoyed two ladies who lived in one of the cottages next to Minster Girls School. I think they were of Eastern European origin. Anyway, they were most intolerant of our games and we were constantly at odds. I can remember that the local window cleaner also lived in Minster Yard North. He was called Dolly Main, and he and his brother cleaned all the windows locally. Both men were hard of hearing, and were always very soberly dressed. They pushed their handcart loaded with various ladders and buckets etc. around the streets of Beverley for many years. There were occasions when people were accidentally locked out of their homes and then Dolly Main would be called upon to gain entry and open the door for them. The Minster Girls School was just that in those days, a busy local primary school. On Sunday afternoons some of the classrooms were used for the Minster Sunday School, run by a group of dedicated ladies who willingly gave their time to a sometimes unwilling pupillage. They all I think were spinster ladies, and I can recall at least three of them, the Misses Fell, and Miss Annie Scoffin. Next to the Girls School, just across a passage that led to the rear of Brentano's Garage was the Minster Parish Room, which in fact was connected to the Vicarage. This room was used for various parish activities, but I remember it most as the venue for the Minster Youth Club.

Coming into Minster Moorgate from the Minster end I recall that Mrs. Winter sold lemonade from her home, which was one of the first row of terraced houses opposite the Minster; then, further along was the entrance to a large garden which belonged to the Vicarage, although not attached to it. Then there was a row of terrace houses which have now been demolished. I remember that Mr. Langley, the cobbler, ran his business from one of these. He was known locally as

'Banger' Langley and was somewhat hard of hearing. Opposite this row of houses was Jack Malton's greengrocery business. This was located through an archway, and the vegetables and fruit were sold from his house. He also had a horse and cart delivery round in Beverley, which his son, Dick, looked after.

My main recollection of Minster Moorgate is, of course, my very first school, Minster Infants. This little school was just opposite Regent Street. I can remember my first day, and my first encounter with school milk when I had some difficulty with the straw, which was something I had not come across before. Miss Walker, our class teacher, soon had me sorted out. Miss Ockleton was the headmistress, and the other class teacher I remember was Miss Drury. It was a only a small school, split up into two buildings separated by the playground. The rear building housed us 'new' children for our first year, and then we all went to classrooms in the main building which fronted onto Minster Moorgate. I was there from 1942 to 1945, which were war years, and now and again the air raid sirens would sound during lessons. When this happened we would all be let out of school and sent home. I remember a school party we had in the garden at the rear of the first-year building. I am sure it was held to celebrate some good wartime news, because we all were given icecream and a badge with wings on. Perhaps it was 'Wings Day'. Anyway, I remember everyone was very happy about it. I learned to read at this school, and I can recall to this day the very first book I read. It was called *Little Black Sambo,* and told of a little boy who, chased by tigers, sought refuge up a tree; the tigers, being angry, ran around and around the tree until they turned to butter, and the little boy was able to return home safely to his family. Playground games were 'Block 123' and 'What time is it, Mr. Wolf?' That little school is now a private house.

Opposite Minster Infants School, on the corner of Regent Street was a small grocery shop, which I think was owned by Miss Owen. Then, further up Minster Moorgate just opposite the Almshouses, was another little shop which sold groceries and sweets and suchlike. Unfortunately I cannot remember who owned it, but in the same row of houses I can remember a gentleman who always stood in the doorway of one of the houses. He was known as Major Good, was quite elderly, had a waxed moustache, and always wore a row of military medals pinned to his waistcoat. I do not know which war he fought in, perhaps it was the Great War or even the Boer War.

Now to St. John Street and Minster Yard South. My paternal

Minster towers viewed from the garden of No. 5 St. John Street. c.1950.

grandparents lived in St. John Street at number five, just opposite the towers and west door of the Minster. My visits to number five were frequent. I knew most of the families in the street too. There were the Oldfields, the Johnsons, the Hodgsons, the Fusseys, the Beaumonts, the Scotts, the Cumins, the Naylors, the Jones, the Wilsons, and the Tanfields. My Grandad's house had a cellar, which was always good for exploring, and also in the garden was an Anderson air raid shelter which featured in many childhood games. The houses in St. John Street with small front gardens all had iron railings and iron gates around the gardens. During the war these railings were removed to contribute to the war effort, and were never replaced. I remember the pathway at the rear of the houses gave access to some very fruitful apple trees and cultivated brambles. There was even a hazel nut tree which bore fruit, so some 'scrumping' certainly took place.

At the junction of Minster Yard South and Long Lane is Baxter's Field. I remember that this field belonged to Mr. Baxter who had a small farm at the rear and side of the Hall Garth, of which there is more later. I can recall that Baxter's Field was often the venue for

The Hall Garth taken shortly before its demolition in March 1957.

circuses and menageries. I think that there is a local bye-law or some ruling that this field must never be built on, and must in perpetuity remain as it is. I hope indeed that this is the case. The Hall Garth was rather a gaunt old house, which had many years before been an inn, and before that a court house. It stood near the north-eastern corner of Baxter's Field. There was a set of stone steps I remember at the side of the house which had long ago been used as an aid to mounting one's horse. I know that the house was occupied when I was a small boy, but it eventually fell into ruin and was demolished in 1957. Interestingly, the Hall Garth is mentioned in the writings of Daniel Defoe. I think that it is sad that both the character and the history of the Hall Garth were ignored. It surely should have been restored to stand as part of Beverley's heritage.

Next to the Hall Garth was the Minster Boys School garden, which fronted onto Minster Yard South up to its junction with Lurk Lane. Lurk Lane in those days was a narrow lane with a row of cottages across the top end and another row on the side opposite the school garden. I remember a communal air raid shelter that stood opposite the first row of cottages. At the end of the lane was the Minster Boys School, which I attended from the age of eight years to eleven years, which would be 1945-1948. For all of us little lads this was 'big' school, and I can recall being somewhat in awe of the 14-year-olds who were at that school and just about to leave to go into work. My years there are recalled as both agreeable and happy, although I did encounter bullying and also my first playground fight, but I allowed neither experience to interfere with my general enjoyment of the second stage of my education. Mr. Grainger was the Headteacher, having just taken over from Mr. 'Dodie' Whitehead, who had just retired before my arrival at the school. My first-year teacher was Miss Maggie Wells, who was sometimes assisted by Mr. Dickie Wynne, who I think had retired once but had returned to help out. He seemed very old. There were more than 40 pupils to a class, all with quite different aspirations as far as education was concerned, but, apart from the odd disruptive pupil, I recall that in the main discipline was good. The use of the wooden ruler across the palm of the hand was a sanction used to good effect on certain pupils, and I was no exception.

Mr. Philip Fussey was one of the second-year teachers. He was the son of one of the local butchers, and had I think fought in the war with the Royal Air Force, and during his lessons he would tell us about his wartime exploits, so his classes were always popular. He also had the knack of making the history that he taught come alive, and I think that it was probably due to him that I have always had an interest in things historical. Mr. Brusby taught English and Music, and sometimes the Head would take us for singing. Two of the songs I remember we used to sing were, *Where e'er you walk*, and *Begone dull care*. What on earth today's children with their 'pop culture' would have made of that, one can but wonder? The other teachers that I remember were Mr. Drewery, who among other subjects taught Art, and Mr. Grayburn, a new teacher who didn't seem to stay with us long. I have a recollection that Mr. Maffin was the school caretaker. Apart from the usual playground games of football and cricket, collecting cigarette cards was one of the games on the go at the time. This involved propping a collectable card against the wall so that all players could take it in turns to knock it down by flicking other cards at it. Whoever knocked the card down also collected all the cards on the floor. This game was also played using the round cardboard bottle tops with the hole in the middle from the school milk supply. The game of 'conkers' was also very popular, and many methods of hardening the chestnuts were tried, including soaking in vinegar, and baking in the oven. Sadly, Minster Boys School was demolished some years ago, and as far as I know no sign of it remains.

The final building in Minster Yard South was the Constitution

Borough of Beverley Education Committee.

MINSTER BOYS' SCHOOL.

SCHOLAR'S REPORT for ___Year___ ended ___August___ 19 48

Name ___WARNES David___ Class ___IV___

Parents are requested to examine carefully the following Report, so that the Children may be encouraged to take interest in their work at School.

Subject.	Marks Possible	Marks Obtained	Remarks on Subject.
Reading	30	17	very neat, fully understood the subject matter
Writing	20	10	when he tries, he can write reasonably
Arithmetic	100	41	He is capable of better things if he would concentrate. 20th in exam.
English Literature Spelling	100	41	Good
(a) Composition Comprehension Test	30	12	Good ideas, spoiled by careless & sometimes wholly exposition
(b)	10		very good understanding
(c) Grammar	10	4	Good knowledge of rules
History	100	72	good year's work. 4th in exam.
Geography	30	68	Good. have gave could compose his work still more
Nature Study and General Knowledge	10	6	Good.
Drawing	100	53	Neat work handy
Handwork	20	4	Fairly good when he tries
	10		

Position in Class ___8th.___ Number in Class ___42___

Average Age of Class ___16 yrs. 11 months___

Explanation of Marks: E.—Excellent; V.G.—Very Good; G.—Good; F.G.—Fairly Good; F.—Fair; B.—Bad or Fail.

CONDUCT AND GENERAL REMARKS. He has ability and intelligence, but unless he is driven hard perpetually, he will not use either. Under the stimulus of a test or exam. he will exert himself, but he is handicapped by his lack of concentration and "woolly-headedness" during ordinary class-work.

He must learn to concentrate and to work for himself on his own _____ Head Teacher.

Philip Fraser _____ Class Teacher.

Minster Boys School report. 1948.

Hall, the entrance to which was in Flemingate. I remember that this hall was used for concerts and exhibitions. It was also used extensively as campaign headquarters by the local Conservative Party during General Elections. I recall that Mr. George Odey was the local Member of Parliament, and I can just remember that his predecessor was Mr. Gurney Braithwaite. The Constitution Hall was demolished many years ago, and it, the Minster Boys School, and the Hall Garth were replaced by the sheltered dwellings and flats complex that we see today.

CHAPTER FIVE

Flemingate, Keldgate and Long Lane

Memories of Flemingate begin for me with the Sun Inn, which fortunately is still with us today, although it has undergone a quite unnecessary name change, like some of the other town hostelries. It was at the Sun Inn that at a very tender age I became acquainted with Hull Brewery mild beer. It was when I was a choirboy. Two or three of us would slip very quietly into what was known then as the Jug and Bottle Department. This was entered through a side door, leading to a very small lobby, which had a tiny hatch from where beer and stout could be purchased discreetly, for home consumption. Sitting in that lobby most evenings was a dear old lady, always dressed in black, taking a glass or two of stout. We would join her occasionally, when our funds permitted it, and she would buy, on our behalf, a half pint of mild. As we were quite small, the landlord could not see us through the hatch so with the old lady's help we got away with it. She was known to us as Grandma Gannon, and I think that she enjoyed our company, for she was a friendly old lady. One of the Sun Inn's later landlords was Mr. Spick.

Next to the Sun Inn was Mr. Jack Ford's papershop. This little newsagent's also sold sweets, and being close to Minster Boys School it did a fair trade in liquorice root, locust beans, and, as I recall, a pink candy stick called a Salsy Bar. Just across the road were two fairly large houses (one was called Beverlac), where a close boyhood friend of that time lived. His name was Michael Haley, and I can recall that we got into quite a few scrapes together. Every week we would swap comics, my *Beano/Dandy* for his *Knockout*. Unfortunately, as our educational paths went in different directions, we gradually lost touch, but those times with Michael are happily remembered. Along from Mr. Ford's shop I can recall a furniture shop, which I think was owned by Mr. Hector Reynolds, a well-known local actor, who took leading roles in many locally produced plays. This shop I think eventually became a used car showroom and business owned by Mr. Tim G. Robson. Next was the Lord Nelson public house followed by two or three small cottages which ran up to the railway crossing, one of which I think was a small shop belonging to Mr. Huggins, a greengrocer. At the other side of the road was Mr. Jack Conway's butcher's shop, and this was close to a ladies' hairdresser on the corner of St. Andrew

Street, belonging to Mrs. Wardrobe. The next business before the railway crossing was a fish and chip shop. I think it was known as the Ideal Fisheries. I remember that it had a large frosted glass window on which was engraved a very large fish.

St. Andrew Street, which is just off Flemingate, was a small street, with houses either side. In those days it just led to the rear of the Minster Boys School playground. I began a course of piano lessons in the front room of Mrs. Hutchins' house in St. Andrew Street, which unfortunately I did not finish. This was no reflection on Mrs. Hutchins who was a very good teacher; rather it was the sound of one's pals playing football in the street outside which somehow disturbed my concentration, so that in the end five-finger exercises lost out to street games, and the half-crown per hour fee, it was decided, would be better spent elsewhere. I had many childhood friends who lived in the St. Andrew Street area, and many childhood adventures were shared with John Taylor, Bill Marshall, Neville Merrington, Charlie and Johnny Ellerington, David Galvin, Raymond Nicholson, Roland Overton, Cecil Egan, and Audrey Richmond, whose dad was the well-known local cricketer, Ted Richmond.

Much of Flemingate was taken up by Richard Hodgson's tannery. This was a huge industrial enterprise which employed many people, producing leather for all manner of products. It extended along most of the eastern side of Flemingate, much of Chantry Lane, and along Priory Road through to St. Nicholas Road. The owners must have been quite philanthropic, as the business had its own recreation ground, with football and cricket pitches, bowling greens and tennis courts. There was Fleming House, too, which was a large social clubhouse. It also had its own ballroom in Priory Road where dances were held most Saturday nights. All these facilities were there for the use of the employees and their families. I can recall the different smells of the tanning process, and some of them, although pretty foul, were an accepted part of the Beverley scene. I can remember seeing the hides as they were moved through the streets to different parts of the factory. Small loads were pulled by hand barrow, and the larger loads were moved by a sort of three-wheeled articulated vehicle. The cabs I remember were painted dark blue, and I think they were called Scamell Horses. The factory had a buzzer which sounded at eight o'clock in the morning, again at twelve noon, an hour later at one o'clock, and finally at five o'clock in the evening. This was a useful indicator to us youngsters playing in the surrounding countryside that it was time to go home. Another memory is of the Hodgson's cricket team entertaining a Yorkshire side, one of whose members was a very youthful Fred Trueman. Although the Hodgson name remains connected to the area, in that there is a smaller chemical industry occupying a small part of the site today, Hodgson's as it was has gone. The main processing area is now a museum, not of tanning, but of Army Transport. Fleming House is now a public house, and the recreational facilities are now owned by the local council.

Further along Flemingate fairly close to Spark Mill Lane I can remember the Scaife family had an icecream business. Spark Mill Lane led past the rear of Hodgson's Recreation Ground, and to open fields. One of these fields was used as a pitch by Beverley United Football club. I remember they played in red and white quartered shirts. Beverley United F.C. is no longer with us today and quite recently I saw that the field was growing a fine crop of peas for freezing. Going along Flemingate towards Potter Hill and Beckside, and just opposite a chapel, was the hall which was the headquarters of the 4th Beverley [Minster] Scout troop, of which fine group of youngsters I was a member, becoming leader of the Kestrel patrol. This hall may have been a school building at one time. The scoutmaster was Mr. Trevor Hopkinson, who was assisted by Mr. Bernard Wharam. I remember that the neckerchiefs were half blue and half white, with the Minster coat of arms embroidered on the back. This was a shield with a bishop's crozier motif. Finally, at the top of Flemingate, there was Mr. Ocky Clark's lodging house, which is there today, although I do not know if it is still in use as a lodging house.

Keldgate holds many boyhood memories. Every day of my Grammar School life I would either walk or cycle up Keldgate on my way to school. Starting at the Minster end I remember the little grocery shop owned by the Misses Constable. Then there was the Ann Routh Hospital where little old ladies lived away their final years in peace and quiet. I used to go with my family to visit Mrs. Grindell, who was one of the residents. She always seemed very snug and content in her little room. Mr. George Odey, the local Member of Parliament and also the chairman of Hodgson's tannery, lived at Keldgate Manor. His well-kept gardens and fishponds, together with his bountiful orchards, were a temptation that for young lads was hard to resist, and many a raid was planned and successfully executed, though sometimes the booty was abandoned in the ensuing chase. Keldgate Manor is now a residential home for the elderly. Incidentally, quite some years before I was born, my Grandma Warnes owned a small baker's shop which was located just before Keldgate Manor.

Opposite the old Grammar School building was Melrose Tannery, which was much smaller than Hodgson's, and I seem to recall that its processes were done more in the open air than in sheds, but that is just an impression, for now it is gone and houses have been built on the site. In one of the houses just on from the tannery lived Mr. Freddie Constable, a well-known local cyclist. Just along from here was Miss Lizzy Monkman's little baker's and grocery shop, which I recall was later taken over by the Loft family. I remember the new Beehive public house being built. It was a Hull Brewery house, and the first landlord was Mr. Bill Grant. Further along and opposite the Lairgate junction is Kitchen Lane, which led to a large area of allotments which ran all the way through to Queensgate, and then on to open fields. My Grandad Warnes had one of those allotments. Towards the top end of Keldgate there was yet another fish and chip shop. I cannot recall who owned it, but I often visited it. I have a vague recollection too of a cobbler's shop just opposite, owned, I think, by Mr. Took.

Keldgate area friends remembered are Michael Bentley, Eric Holtby, Stanley Shaw, Peter Wrigglesworth, Brian Marshall, Dick Loft, Tommy Cole, Don Perry, Tony Oxtoby and Adrian Senior.

In early childhood and as a young boy, Long Lane was a semi-paradise for me, leading as it did to the countryside. It was my good fortune that my maternal grandparents owned a small farm in Long Lane where I often stayed for long periods, and it was from there that I was able to be involved in the adventures, exploits, and expeditions that living there presented to a young boy and his friends. Long Lane is aptly named, leading from the Minster to Woodmansey, so, to begin at the Minster end: Mr. Fred Osgerby and his family lived in one of the row of cottages opposite Baxter's Field. I have mentioned Uncle Fred previously. I recall Minster Avenue was an unmade road with a small row of cottages down one side leading to Mr. Laffy Ewen's smallholding and orchard. The orchard presented us with many 'scrumping' opportunities. From the south-western corner of Baxter's Field as far as England Springs there is a row of several pairs of semi-detached houses, where in those days, long ago, many of my friends lived. Opposite these houses was a belt of trees which surrounded one of Mr. Odey's grazing pastures. This belt of trees, or plantation as we called it, with its well established rookery, was not just a playground to us: it gave us our first understanding of nature and natural history, for it was here that our first birdnesting expeditions took place, and our egg collections were started. I know that these days collecting birds eggs is illegal, but we youngsters had our rules when 'bod nesting' (using the vernacular was perhaps a rule too). For instance, when a nest was found the location was always kept secret, and usually never more than one egg was taken, and if the 'awd bod' was on the nest it was not disturbed. Blowing the eggs was a delicate operation as I recall, as having pierced each end of the egg with a thorn from a hawthorn bush, one had to blow pretty hard, yet with great care to remove the contents. Sometimes the egg would be 'gollified', which meant it had a chick close to hatching in it, so if this was thought to be the case the egg would not be pricked and would be replaced. During the nesting season our arms would be covered in scratches from hand to shoulder, and falls from trees were not uncommon. Special memories of those times are the finding of a cuckoo's egg in a dunnock's nest, and acquiring a kestrel's egg with its orange-reddish markings. We would keep our eggs in cardboard boxes or wooden cases, labelling them and laying them on a bed of cotton wool. There was pride and some skill in what we did then, and, although very young, I feel that we acted carefully and responsibly. The field which that plantation surrounded is now a housing development, and what is left of the plantation seems to be threatened.

From the first bridge at England Springs, a little cinder track led through to the railway line and Sparkmill Lane. Just up this track was Mrs. Fenby's house and field. Mrs. Fenby was well-known as a breeder of Bedlington terriers. As you walked up the cinder track the Bedlingtons would run alongside you, just inside the fence and bark. Mrs. Fenby often used to hold dog shows at her England Springs home for the local children. These little shows were never very serious affairs, but I think were rather meant to pass her love of animals on to us children. They were very popular. I can remember the water in England Springs was usually running clear, although in February it could be very deep and cloudy. We would collect frog spawn from it and catch tadpoles and newts, and in late spring and summer the kingcups flourished, just like giant buttercups on the water. Passing Mrs. Fenby's we came to a field. This, the first field, we all called 'Foggy Field', and the next field we called 'Seggy Field'. Apart from football and cricket, many childhood games were played in these and the surrounding fields. I remember too we gathered lots of mushrooms from those fields in the morning mists of early autumn. Back then into Long Lane and at a small brick bridge the springs divided into dykes at either side of the road, the right hand dyke branching down Black Lane, which was a small cinder track leading to more fields and open countryside. At intervals along the length of Black Lane dyke grew the common osier willow trees. These willows were not too tall and were good to climb. I have a recollection of the willow sticks being cut and gathered, perhaps for use in supporting vegetables on the nearby allotments. This little area is now further threatened by the proposed Figham link road.

A paddock's length along from Black Lane, and set back off the road, was Willow Croft. This was the small farmstead belonging to my maternal grandparents, where I spent many happy hours of my childhood. The house, which had two south-facing bay windows catching the sun, had a warm and friendly feel, especially in the evenings when the oil lamps were lit, for there was no electricity there then, and with the smell of the oil and in the gentle warm glow of the light, I felt very secure. Just through green-painted iron gates was the dairy where my Grandma Osgerby made curd and

other dairy products for sale at the farm gate and in the town. I can remember the muslin curd bags, the wooden butter pats and the shiny metal separator that was manually operated to take the cream from the milk. Further along was the cowshed where Grandad did the milking, and there was also a pigsty nearby. I have so many memories of Willow Croft, of being allowed to ride back from the fields to the farm on the dapple-grey carthorse with old Codge, the farm dog, trotting behind, of haymaking, of helping my Grandad bring the cows home for

The author at Willow Croft. c.1939.

milking and helping my Grandma to feed the chickens. I can remember too the orchard with its sweet apple trees. One particular vivid recollection concerns my one and only encounter with a German bomber. I can remember that I would have been about three or four years old at the time, so it would be 1940 or '41. I was by the main gates when I heard the loud droning of engines in the sky. It was really all over in a flash, but I recall looking up and seeing about a field away, and over the Hull to Beverley railway line, a big black aircraft flying very low. I can remember that at this moment I was swept up by my Grandma, and she hurled both of us into the cupboard under the stairs. She was crying, and I remember the house shook as some bombs exploded in Beverley. In the darkness of that cupboard the noise was more like a 'crump' than a bang. Of course, I didn't realise at the time what all the fuss was about, but it was an event I have never forgotten.

My Grandad died in 1944 and my Grandma kept the farm going for a time. I remember that she employed Mr. Jim Evans to help her run the farm, and he used to let me help him sometimes. Jim Evans lived in Queensgate, and I can recall visiting his family with my mother and grandma. In his garden shed he had made little wooden models of men doing various jobs, such as sawing logs, chopping sticks, digging the garden, and other routine tasks. All these little chaps were hand-painted in detail, had moveable heads, arms and legs, and were connected by a series of pulleys and cogs to a windmill on the roof of the shed, so that, when the wind blew, each worker would energetically set about his task. It was a wonderful sight to see this little hive of industry, so skilfully made by Jim Evans. I do not know if many people knew of his skill, as he was by nature a very quiet chap. I often wondered what became of that little tableau. In a few years the little farmstead was sold,

Family group at Willow Croft. c.1943.

54

becoming for a while a market garden and eventually the garden centre it is today. Things are much changed in that area now, and I do not condemn any of the enterprise that has effected the changes, although, when I pass by Willow Croft today, I am so glad that I knew it in those far-off days, and wonder if it is able to feel my remembrance of that special time.

To continue then, in Long Lane, just past Willow Croft, a track led down to some sheds, and a barn, where Mr. Joe Bird kept a few sheep. Then, further along and on the other side of the road was Black House, which was mainly a pig farm owned by Mr. Seymour. Almost opposite and just across the railway line was Mr. Voase's dairy farm, which we called Beverley Parks. A further track led off Long Lane to White Hall farm which was owned by Mr. Barrett. I can recall one of our boyhood expeditions led us through White Hall farm and on as far as Jillywood, where a certain 'Old Man Childs', who was the local gamekeeper, sent us packing with more than a flea in our ear. The next house in Long Lane belonged to Mr. Jolley and Mrs. Jolley. This was a tidy little cottage by the roadside, and I can remember all the flowers in the garden around the house. Today that little cottage stands sadly derelict. Crossing the railway line and just after the next bend in the lane was what we knew as 'Murder Pool'. I can recall this being a scary place, as local legend told of the murder long ago of a young woman by a soldier. We all kept well clear of the place just in case it was haunted. The site was later used to store scrap metal and old cars, and was an eyesore for many years. The lane ended where it met the main Hull road, just opposite Thearne Lane. My sister and I used to cycle from our home to buy our pet mice and rabbits from a Mr. Grindell who bred such things at his home in Thearne. That then is just a little of Long Lane and its fields. It truly was a special place, not just for me but for all the youngsters who roamed its paths and meadows, who knew the nature of the place, who knew where the waterhen lay, where the flycatcher nested, who saw the hedgerows bloom in the spring, and who marvelled at the shortlived blushing dog rose, the cuckoo pint, and wild autumn mushrooms.

Long Lane friends remembered are Aubrey Perry, Kenny Oakes, Brian and June Vincent, Audrey Everingham, Tony and Trevor Galvin, Gerald Thompson, Brian and Margaret Robinson, John Turgoose, Tom Waddy, Vanessa Voase and Ron Mawer. Many others previously mentioned in this book also had childhood connections with Long Lane.

CHAPTER SIX

The Westwood, the Grammar School, and here and there

Family picnics are among my first recollections of the Westwood, sitting among the buttercups and daisies in Union Bushes eating sandwiches. I can remember one summer's day when we had a picnic on 'Hill 60', and from the top we were able to watch the horseracing on the Hurn. We knew all the best places to pitch stumps for a game of cricket, and Union Bushes was a large playground for all us youngsters, with climbable trees, hills, tracks and even small cliffs. Lime Kilns was similar, but much smaller. The clumps of gorse bushes that were dotted around would always yield a lost golf ball or two, and you could guarantee to find the nest of the scribblefinch there. Burton Bushes was a special place with lots of wildlife to see and hear. In the springtime there were the bluebells, and the wood rang with bird song. On hot summer days it would be cool in the pathways beneath the trees, and in late summer and early autumn we would gather brambles and watch the grey squirrels in the trees. It wasn't fenced in those days, and the Westwood cattle would roam through it freely. I think that most of the cattle that grazed on the Westwood pastures then were milking cows, and they would walk gently and sedately to their milking parlours every day. One was Mr. Charlie Thompson's in Cartwright Lane, and the other one I remember was near the York Road gatehouse, just opposite Willow Grove. There were always lots of sheep grazing on the pastures too. Nowadays it seems mainly to be young bullocks.

I can recall that there were two very good ponds on the Westwood, both of which are no longer there. One was at Anti Mill, which is now the Golf Club car park, and the other was on the Hurn, close to the five-furlong start on the racecourse. We would catch red-breasted sticklebacks and newts in abundance from these two ponds, taking them in jam jars to our home-made aquaria. Today I would not know where to go locally to catch a stickleback, which is very sad. Whenever it snowed it seemed that all the children of the town could be found on the Westwood with all manner of home-made toboggans. I recall that 'Hill 60' was the longest run and fairly slow, 'Niagara'' in Union Bushes was fast, with bumps and tight turns, and the 'Cinder Track' was fast and narrow. There were other slopes, too, but I cannot recall them having names. I think that 'Hill 60' was named after a battle on the Ypres front in 1915 where the East Yorkshire Regiment saw action in fighting successfully for possession of the hill. There is also 'Majuba Hill', the 15th hole of the golf course, which was named after a Boer War battle. During the last war large areas of the Westwood were ploughed up and cereals were grown. It is still just possible to tell where these areas are, because the grass used to replant the pastures after the war seemed to be a much coarser type than the original. In those days you would see the racehorses training on the Tan Gallop. This was a special track in the area between Westwood Road and Newbald Road, about a mile in length, and about three yards wide which was filled with the oak bark waste from the tanneries. This was almost an all-weather medium for horses to train on, and must have saved the turf from damage. Although the track is still there today, all the oak chippings have long since gone, and I am sure that it is no longer seriously used by racehorses. I remember the two well-known local trainers, Pat Taylor and Snowy Gray. You could see their strings of horses almost every day, making their way up York Road to the Westwood for exercise. They were so much part of the Beverley scene in those days.

The golf course took up a large part of the Westwood. The clubhouse of the Beverley and East Riding Golf Club was in those days a small wooden affair attached to Anti Mill. As young boys we all managed to acquire some very second-hand golf clubs, all with hickory shafts as I recall, and with names instead of numbers. Mashies, Niblicks, Brassies and Spoons were the tools of our trade then. Our golf balls were either 'finds', or supplied by an old gentleman by the name of Dick Lundie who was quite a well-known local character. He lived in a small cottage in Keldgate, and spent much of his time searching the Westwood for lost golf balls which he sold to us for a 'tanner' each. We used to literally help ourselves to as many rounds of golf as we could manage during the school holidays. Surprisingly, this did not seem to be discouraged by the members, or by the greenkeepers, and, provided we deferred to the members who were playing at the time, we were able to have many hours of free golf, when we learned the basic skills, the rules and the etiquette of the game. I can remember at this time caddies were employed by some of the members, and the club ran what they called an Artisans' Section, for the craftsmen of the town. This section was housed in Anti Mill. I can recall marvelling at the skills of Mr. George Ash who was a very famous local golfer, winning many golfing honours. In those days there were no fences around the greens, and cow pats were removed daily by the two greenkeepers. The pleasure of the game has remained with me since those early days, and I was able to enjoy the privilege of membership of the Beverley club for a number of years until working commitments limited my time.

As the town of Beverley has expanded over the years, one of the major changes to be seen is in the education system. It would seem that, here as elsewhere, local schools have changed not only to accommodate population expansion, but also to accommodate certain political views, which to me seemed to have been based either on envy or elitism. Politicians, I think, should leave teaching to the teachers. That said, however, I can only say that my school days were indeed some of the happiest days of my life, and in that regard I really do feel fortunate. At the age of 11, I left many of my school friends at Minster Boys and for the next six years I was a pupil at Beverley Grammar School. Becoming a first former was not without its initial stresses, but I was again fortunate in that I had a choirboy pal who was in the second form, so I knew something of what to expect, and reading the works of Frank Richards and Thomas Hughes had given me an idea too, so I was perhaps luckier than some in that it was only a minor shock to the system. Even the feared initiation ceremonies proved to be more myth than fact. The first form classrooms in the lower school had the stuffed heads of animals displayed on the wall. I recall that there were leopards, panthers, and bears hanging there. I do not know where they came from, only that I found them quite interesting, as I suppose any young boy would.

So there I was, with the uniform of black cap with a white roundel and badge, a black blazer also with badge, grey flannels, initially short, grey socks with black and white tops, and a black and white horizontally striped tie. I was aware of the financial burden all this placed on my parents, and today's parents, no doubt, will feel similar strains in providing the designer clothing that is demanded now. This uniform, the first of many disciplines, was to be worn to and from school at all times, and, should one meet a master in the street, then the cap must be raised to him, and so very quickly we all learned the many school rules. The first formers were split into two groups, the A's and the B's. If you were put into an A form group then you were perceived to have more academic potential than those in the B form group. I was put into the B form group, and there I remained throughout my entire Grammar School education. I had no quarrel with this as it seemed to me that we B formers were generally able to play more football and cricket, and I was happy with that. Also, there were very few transfers of pupils between groups after the first year, so perhaps those initial perceptions were the right ones.

Mr. J. J. G. Walkinton was the Headmaster during my time at the school. I can remember well his morning walk from his house in the school grounds to his office, wearing his cap and gown, with books under his arm. All the masters wore gowns, and I seem to remember that hoods, too, were sometimes worn at the daily assembly. The school was steeped in its own sense of history and tradition, and I for one was glad to embrace both, although again, it is only some *thirty* and *forty* and *fifty* years on that one truly appreciates being part of that scene. The masters were a group of learned and dedicated men who did have some success in certain subjects as far as my personal education was concerned; the fact that in some very important subjects I was found wanting was entirely my own fault. The masters then, who did their best for me were Mr. Whiteley, Mr. Harrold, Mr. Needham, Mr. Walmsley, Mr. Candler, Mr. Driver, Mr. Wilson, Mr. Lack, the Rev. Langton, Mr. Smith, Mr. Archer, Mr. Barratt, Mr. Black, Mr. Morris, Mr. Rodgers, and Mr. Long. Other masters who were at the school at the time but who did not teach me were Mr. Bradfield, Mr. Rogers, Mr. Beswick and Miss Curtis. Class sizes up to and including the fourth year were about 30, dropping to 20 in the fifth year. Disciplinary sanctions were the imposition of lines, detention, and the cane, which was administered only by the headmaster. I confess to experiencing all three. I remember that a task given to us during the Easter holidays was to write an Empire Essay. This, most of us found somewhat onerous, but we generally found something to write about the British Empire which satisfied the powers that were. I wonder, do the pupils of today have an EEC Essay to write?

There were four houses within the school, Conington, Minster, Fisher and School, which engendered a lively competitive spirit. Sporting activities were encouraged, although by today's standards some of the facilities were pretty basic. The playing fields and gardens were well maintained by Mr. Potter and his staff. Various extra-curricular clubs were organised within the school, and I was a member of two, the Birdwatchers' Club, and the Photographic Society. There was a school tuckshop, which was open during the first morning break. I remember well the delicious rock cakes and iced buns sold there. It was located down by the junior changing rooms, near the school gates. The school boilerman and caretaker was a gentleman called Curly. I cannot remember his surname, which is a bit unusual as everyone at the school was addressed by their surname. I think also that the chap who ran the tuckshop also had a caretaking role. In Sloe Lane there were two small shops which all the pupils of the school patronised. The first one was about a third of the way up Sloe Lane from the school, and I only knew it as Harry's. Harry, the proprietor, sold fizzy drinks, Vantas, in particular, along with the usual schoolboy requirements in the confectionery line. The other little shop was at the end of Sloe Lane, at its junction with Cartwright Lane. I note that it is still used by today's pupils. Then I think it was owned by Mr. Holmes. My best friend at the school was Jim Waddington. We got into many a pickle together both in and out of school, but always in the best possible humour. That then is just a flavour of my Grammar School days. There are so many more memories of that time that perhaps, when I am seeking *solace* in my old age, all the remembrances of my *nurtured youth* will be brought to mind and recorded. In the meantime I can say with certainty that the years I spent at the school did benefit me in later life, and I count my time there as a blessing.

Finally now, before I forget, this brief collection of times remembered is brought to a close with some random 'here and there' memories of the town. For instance, during those times, industries other than those already mentioned flourished in Beverley and made significant contributions to the local economy. I well remember Barker and Lee Smith, makers of animal feedstuffs, with their premises alongside Beverley Beck, on which they received raw material by barge. Of particular interest to us youngsters were those barges carrying monkey nuts, as sometimes we had the opportunity to take samples. In Holme Church Lane there was the ropery which I think was owned by Halls Barton. Then on the River Hull was the shipyard, a very busy place in those far-off days. It was owned by Cook, Welton and Gemmell and I can recall that it built many deep-sea trawlers for the Hull fishing industry. We used to go to watch the ships being launched.

First & Last Editions

England's Second-Hand Bookshops

Gordon Allan

THE *Alpha* PRESS

BRIGHTON • PORTLAND

2 4 6 8 10 9 7 5 3 1

First published 2003, in Great Britain by
THE ALPHA PRESS
PO Box 2950
Brighton BN2 5SP

and in the United States of America by
THE ALPHA PRESS
5824 N.E. Hassalo St.
Portland, Oregon 97213-3644

British Library Cataloguing in Publication Data
A CIP catalogue record for this book is available from the British Library.

Library of Congress Cataloging-in-Publication Data applied for.
Allan, Gordon, 1934–
First and last editions : England's second-hand bookshops /
Gordon Allan.
p. cm.
Includes index.
ISBN 1-898595-41-0 (acid-free paper)
1. Antiquarian booksellers—England. 2. Book collectors—England.
3. Book collecting—England. I. Title.

Z326 .A44 2003
381'.45002'0942—dc21
2002153083

Typeset and designed by G&G Editorial, Brighton
Printed MPG Books Ltd, Bodmin, Cornwall
This book is printed on acid-free paper.